DECOLONISATION & AFTER

DECOLONISATION & AFTER
THE FUTURE OF THE THIRD WORLD

Edited by
Bruno Kreisky & Humayun Gauhar

South Publications
London

South Publications
New Zealand House
80 Haymarket
London SW1Y 4TS

© Third World Foundation 1987

British Cataloguing in Publication Data
Kreisky, Bruno
Decolonisation and After:
The Future of the Third World
1 Developing countries – Economic conditions
I Title 11 Gauhar, Humayun
330.9172'4   HC59.7
ISBN 0 907962 41 6
Cover designed by
Banks and Miles, 1 Tranquil Vale, London SE3
Printed in Great Britain by
Biddles Ltd., Guildford, Surrey.

Contents

Appendix

Introduction

Bruno Kreisky and Humayun Gauhar

In 1985 many countries in the Third World celebrated a special anniversary marking their freedom from colonial rule. For most of these countries this occasion gave rise to reflections upon their experiences since gaining independence and the trials and tribulations associated with regaining control of one's own destiny.

Except in a few cases, the political decolonisation process has long been completed. However, few of the former colonies were well prepared for self-determination at the time they gained independence. The mismatch between the constitutions that were handed down by colonial rulers or drawn up after protracted negotiations on the one hand, and the prevailing social structures on the other hand, undermined the viability of democratic government. As a result we have witnessed a dramatic erosion of democratic principles in the South, and the appearance and spreading of authoritarian forms of government in many parts of the developing world. In addition, asymmetric economic interdependence is merely a hollow concept without a greater voice for the developing countries within the world economic community.

To mark this twenty-fifth anniversary of the independence of many Third World countries the Vienna Institute for Development and 'South—The Third World Magazine' jointly sponsored a conference entitled 'Decolonisation and After—The Future of the Third World' (Vienna, 7–8 October 1985). This conference concerned itself not only with presenting the experiences of African, Asian, Caribbean and Latin American countries, but also provided a forum for some of the visionary ideas that have been put forward for securing and strengthening the self-determination of these states.

It was in the foremost Hapsburg palace (the Hofburg) that the VID-South conference assembled—in the Baroque splendour of the Redoutensaal ballroom. However, the serious tone of Bruno Kreisky's opening address of welcome was a jolting reminder to the large and distinguished international audience that grinding world poverty and not the tuneful cadences of Strauss waltzes were to be the concern of the gathering and one realised the real reason for the choice of Vienna. Kreisky dominated Austrian political life for over a quarter of a century; he was Foreign Minister from 1959–66 and Federal Chancellor of the Republic for fourteen years until his retirement in 1983.

Long before it became fashionable to do so, Kreisky took up the cause of the Third World; in July 1962, he convened a conference on the theme of 'Economic Cooperation and Partnership' to discuss how the international community could be alerted to the needs of the under-developed areas of the world. The Vienna Declaration on Cooperation for Development adopted at that meeting was complemented by the foundation of the VID with the support of Jawaharlal Nehru. Kreisky has strenuously supported the work of the VID over the years, and it was the sharing of the concerns of VID and a recognition of Kreisky's leadership in moving Austria towards 'a bridge-building role between North and South, establishing channels of communication with patience and understanding' (to quote the second speech of welcome from Humayun Gauhar) that led to the planning of a joint meeting by VID and *South*.

Kreisky pointed out—as Chancellor Fred Sinowatz was to also—that 1985 was a year of anniversaries; in particular, the twenty-fifth anniversary of the founding of VID was soon to be celebrated. In the 1960s there was a widespread confidence that the UN was capable of forwarding cooperative policies between the Western industrialised countries and those newly-independent territories beginning then to be known as 'the Third World of under-development'. That confidence had now diminished but the tasks set out by the VID Declaration remained as urgent as ever; indeed, the plight of the Third World was far worse than he could have ever contemplated in the early days of the VID. The Federal Chancellor then welcomed the conference participants on behalf of the Government of Austria and paid tribute to the manifold contributions of Bruno Kreisky to national and international public life. Humayun Gauhar had reminded them of the thirtieth anniversary of the Bandung Conference and Kreisky had spoken of the birth of VID. He, as Chancellor, saw 1985 as 'the year of contemporary history' for Austria: the fortieth anniversary of the end of the Second World War and the foundation of the Second Austrian Republic and the thirtieth anniversary of the Austrian State Treaty and the admission of the Republic to membership of the UN in December 1955. Yet with all this to celebrate, it was not a time for reflection—it was a time for re-orientation of Austria's role; she had never been a colonial power and had always enjoyed a special relationship with the Third World. As socialists and democrats the Austrian government could offer solidarity to those who looked for an escape from poverty. The days of colonialism may be numbered, warned the Chancellor, but it is reappearing in a different form, the neo-colonialism of economic dependence, under which sovereign countries were not always masters of their own fate.

The five guest speakers who then addressed the conference spoke of the experience of the post-1945 years from the perspective of their own area of the Third World: Africa, the Caribbean, Latin America, China and Asia. Amir Jamal—then Minister of State in the Office of the President of Tanzania—concentrated on the theme that political independence marked the beginning of the struggle of the former colonies rather than the end. In the 1960s it seemed possible that economic development could steadily proceed whilst indigenous infrastructures were built up to replace the colonial institutional inheritance; in the 1970s, that possibility was destroyed by the appearance of widespread inflation in the industrialised countries, the sharp increases in the price of oil, the abandonment of fixed exchange rates, the emasculation of development aid and adverse terms of trade for Third World primary products. The wheels of the engine of growth gradually sank deeper in the mud. The only rational and effective option left to the Third World was to collaborate with the medium-sized industrialised countries rather than with the superpowers and those closely associated with them in order to establish a more equitable distribution of power and wealth. Prosperity pre-empted by a few, Jamal concluded, offers only the prospect of global despair.

The contribution of Michael Manley—the former Prime Minister of Jamaica—echoed the apocalyptic pessimism of Kreisky and Jamal, as he remarked that the confident calls of the 1970s for a New International Economic Order (NIEO) had given way in the 1980s 'to a scramble for survival as the tactics of crisis management replaced the strategies of development ... as borrowed money became first, a means of survival, then, because of its cost, a new cause of disaster ... as the Common Fund languishes on the shelves of UNCTAD ... and the International Monetary Fund (IMF) presides over one social disaster after another.' He urged the replacement of 'the politics of expectations' by 'the politics of mobilisation' in which the peoples of the Third World should together compel the convening of an international conference of debtors and creditors at which the reorganisation of the World Bank and the IMF should be discussed in terms of fundamental reforms in decision taking, lending capacity and basic decision-making.

Gabriel Valdes—president of the Christian Democratic Party of Chile, the former Foreign Minister of Chile in the 1960s and closely associated with the United Nations Development Programme (UNDP) in the 1970s—concentrated on the crisis of democracy in Latin America and developed Jamal's theme of neo-colonial economic dependence and the burden of the inheritance of former regimes. However, there was more than economic dependency in Latin America. There was also cultural and political dependency, and he reminded the conference of the saying that 'That which our forefathers have done, holds us in bond for the future.' He traced successive crises in Latin

America from the 1930s onwards and showed how they had lasting effects on the economic and social structures of the region. A factor not to be ignored was the baleful influence of the USA on the domestic policies of the Latin American countries, as present today as ever it was. There was also the almost endemic presence of military dictatorship in Brazil, Uruguay, Argentina, Ecuador, Bolivia and his own country of Chile and their inveterate suppression of human rights. Turning to consider principal trends in the economies of the region, he chose for special mention the effect of fluctuating exchanges rates (as did Manley earlier) and ended by discussing the grave problem of external debt and the political possibilities for coping with its consequences.

The address of He Liliang, a Counsellor in the Ministry of Foreign Affairs in Beijing, attracted special attention from the conference, eager as they were to hear of post-Mao structural reforms in the People's Republic of China. In a detailed presentation, she explained that the main purposes of the reforms were to relax rigid state control over the management of enterprises, to give more emphasis to 'the law of value and the role of the market' and 'to eliminate absolute egalitarianism in our distribution system'. The reforms had resulted in greater enthusiasm from the peasants in their productive work, a marked increase in the supply of agricultural produce and a rapid rise in the income of the rural population; in turn, there was a greater mobility between the industrial and agricultural sectors which further facilitated the development of the overall national economy. She ended by assuring the conference that there would be no restoration of capitalism, that the nature of China's social and economic foundations would remain socialist and that 'the bourgeoisie as a class will never re-emerge in China.'

The last of the papers dealing with reviews of post-colonial experience was given by Altaf Gauhar, who drew on his long experience in public life from the days of British India, in independent Pakistan and the newly-emergent Bangladesh. What was striking about the contributions of Jamal, Manley, Valdes and Gauhar was the prophetic tone; they represented an apocalyptic jeremiad which was saved from despair by a determination to reverse present historical trends. A secondary theme was that political independence did not bring with it the social and economic liberation that was the motive power for nationalist movements during the colonial period. In his review of the post-imperial history of the Indian sub-continent, Gauhar described how national-ist expectations of revolutionary change (*Inqilab*) were dashed:

It did not take long for the people to discover that all that had been changed was the colour of their masters ... independence brought little change and they remained chained to the same British-style institutions which the ruling elites manipulated and controlled to perpetuate their own advantages ... The British-style institutions and the structure of the ruling class has largely remained unchanged ... For the masses the achievement of independence was the end of their struggle and also the end of their dreams ... nationalism could not serve either as a cover to conceal economic and social disparities nor hold back the tides of regional autonomous pressures ... when cultural homogeneity and truly national consciousness failed to evolve, people began to revert to the security of their traditional parochial and class identities ... The seeds of disintegration in the subcontinent were all sown in the colonial period. They are now coming to bitter fruition.

He ended by repeating Jamal's warning not to rely on the succour of the superpowers, but put it in even stronger terms: 'The superpowers have imposed on the globe a regime which can only be described as "nuclear *apartheid*". The superpowers belong to a world apart and they hold all other nations in thrall.' The theme of interdependence and the need for cooperation among the Third World countries which was raised by Kreisky and developed by all the speakers at this conference was once more forcefully expressed: 'Unity and collective action by all nations of the world has now become an imperative of survival ...'

The second day of the conference was devoted to the theme 'prospects for the future', Bruno Kreisky opening with a second and more detailed exposition on 'North–South cooperation'. He was followed by Professor Louis Emmerij with a characteristically forceful discussion of 'recovery and development'. In the third presentation, international financial institutions suffered a direct frontal assault from Teresa Hayter asking 'Is reform of the World Bank possible?' and the conference papers were concluded on a forward-looking note by Professor Janez Stanovnik who spoke on 'towards a new internationalism', without feeling the need for a question-mark.

Kreisky began in challenging style by questioning the formulation of the concept of the New International Economic Order; very often, it seemed to him, the calls for an NIEO were based on unrealistic proposals and cited the failure of the Cancún meeting—concerned with the removal of the impasse over the provision of development aid—as an instance of this. To meet the sharp deterioration in the condition of the Third World countries in the early 1980s, he suggested a concentration on the infrastructural needs of these countries. He dealt in some detail with the need for developments in the fields of transport, water-management and telecommunications and cited the commissioning of a feasibility study by the VID on an inter-state railway system in Africa. There was also the problem of combating unemployment;

prosperity did not always increase employment, for investment was often directed towards labour-saving ends and diminishing labour-intensive situations. He stressed the importance of bringing the concerns of the conference to the notice of the general public and suggested that the message be that their own self-interest was threatened by crises in a world becoming increasingly interdependent. We should learn from the recent successes of the European peace movement in arousing general concern. He ended by emphasising the need for systematic study of the philosophy and theory of development problems against which practical programmes could be tested and new ideas generated.

Louis Emmerij—then Rector of the Institute of Social Studies, The Hague and now Director of the OECD Development Centre in Paris—managed to find yet another anniversary to mention and opened with congratulatory remarks to *South* on its fifth year of publication. His speech which referred to and commented on the contributions of Kreisky, Manley and Jamal demonstrated another remarkable feature of the conference proceedings; namely, the way in which all the speeches were interlinked and interconnected and made up a coherent and consistent body of thought, a rare event in international gatherings. He talked of the way in which the political acceptability of ideas can rapidly change and that new ideas should be discussed not in terms of their current acceptability but in terms of need and relevance; the impossible can soon become the current orthodoxy. In the OECD countries, there must be changes in the decision-making processes, there must be an international stimulation of demand by a massive transfer of resources, and there must be a solution of the unemployment problem. He saw two major choices that face the contemporary world: to continue with a global international division of labour or to move in the direction of regional divisions of labour. He ended by calling for a simultaneous recovery in the world economy rather than waiting for the locomotive of the USA to pull the wagons of the world behind it. Europe in terms of its population and its economies is a world power with a regional product close to that of the United States and larger than the Soviet Union and Japan; it should bestir itself and take the lead in world economic recovery. It should act like a superpower and not like a laggard sheep.

Teresa Hayter set out her position and relentlessly argued the case for its validity. First, the World Bank is an instrument of the foreign economic policies of the USA and its major Western allies; its over-riding objective was the promotion and preservation of the capitalist system in the Third World. Second, the World Bank gave preference to the interests of capitalism in the major Western Powers over those of capitalism in the Third World. Third, this situation will remain unchanged unless there are radical changes in the governments of the major Western powers, including that of the USA. The structure of decision-making in the World Bank and its dependence upon private capital markets for funds made early reform an unlikely prospect.

Professor Stanovnik, in a wide-ranging address which drew on earlier themes of the conference and discussed them with reference to the historical experience of Europe over the last hundred years, ended by calling for radical changes in the existing patterns of development, the promotion of the idea and the practice of 'collective self-reliance' and the construction of a 'new alliance', a new association between North and South and rich and poor.

The conference chairman, Thorvald Stoltenberg—Chairman of the North-South Commission (Committee of the Whole) of the UN during 1978-79 and a leading member of the Norwegian Labour Party—summed up the conference proceedings by suggesting that they provided for guidance what might be called 'The Vienna Way' which comprised seven practical action-oriented proposals that should be implemented:

> *First*, the recognition and acceptance of the implications of 'common interest' in the resolution of what the Brandt Commission called a 'common crisis';
>
> *Second*, the need to foster, encourage, extend and promote economic and social democracy in the countries of the Third World;
>
> *Third*, the strengthening of people-to-people cooperation;
>
> *Fourth*, the revival of multilateralism, especially in the UN, and the reform of the World Bank and the International Monetary Fund;
>
> *Fifth*, the extension of cooperation between the Third World and 'the like-minded' (such as the Scandinavian countries);
>
> *Sixth*, the strengthening of South-South cooperation and the creation of a South Secretariat; and,
>
> *Seventh*, a massive transfer of resources within the 'one world' community.

Welcome addresses

1. Humayun Gauhar

Mr Chancellor, Excellencies, ladies and gentlemen

I have the honour to join His Excellency Dr Bruno Kreisky in welcoming our distinguished guest speakers as well as our guest participants.

It is a matter of great pride and honour for *South* magazine to co-sponsor the seminar on 'Decolonisation and After—The Future of the Third World'—with the Vienna Institute for Development. We are also greatly honoured that the Chancellor of Austria, His Excellency Dr Fred Sinowatz, is here with us today to inaugurate the seminar and deliver the opening address. Your presence, Mr Chancellor, is most significant because it is a testimony to Austria's deep interest in North–South affairs.

When we set out some seven months ago to work on the idea of a joint seminar between the Vienna Institute for Development and *South* magazine, we did not anticipate the extraordinary response in terms of attendance that we see in this beautiful baroque ballroom. We planned for a hundred participants and today we have over two hundred and fifty gathered here. This in itself is evidence of the importance of the subject on our agenda.

Today and tomorrow we discuss the impact of the decolonisation process, some twenty-five years after the momentum of the 1960s which spawned so many new independent states. We are here to learn about these states' experiences of decolonisation and to assess whether the former metropolitan powers have shed their feelings of guilt as they themselves become more preoccupied with their own political and economic problems. Of equal importance is to learn from our speakers their evaluation of the lessons on the decolonisation process.

There are a number of reasons why this time and place are appropriate for a discussion on decolonisation and the future of the Third World. It is now thirty years since the Bandung Conference, and twenty-five years since the decolonisation process reached its peak in 1960. In most Third World countries, a generation has passed since independence; it is a generation which has seen the turbulent transfer of power, the fading of initial hopes for rapid economic development, and the successive application of many approaches to the problems of underdevelopment with indifferent results. In most countries of the Third World, leadership has passed—sometimes violently—from the generation which won independence to a new group of leaders educated in the post-colonial environment. These new leaders are looking for new approaches. It is appropriate, then, that we meet now, in 1985, to take stock of the failures and successes of a generation, and compare experiences from three continents.

It is fitting, too, that we do this in Vienna, for in the same year as the meeting in Bandung—1955—Austria re-emerged from the shadows of the Cold War as a sovereign, neutral nation, her neutrality guaranteed by the State Treaty. Since that time, Austria has been able to play a bridge-building role between East and West, and, more recently, between North and South, establishing channels of communication with patience and understanding.

Here, then, at a crossroads between East and West, North and South, past and future, we are reflecting on our experiences and evaluating our prospects. Today's speakers, though they come from different regions, all share a common perspective, a Third World perspective.

We at *South* magazine grapple daily with the expression 'Third World'. The states which make up the Third World are often referred to collectively, as if they were one region. Yet what we now call the Third World is in fact most of the world. *South* recognises the dangers of lumping such a large and diverse number of peoples into one category; to do so is to ignore the uniqueness of each culture. But to recognise the Third World's rich diversity does not deprive the concept of its significance. The Third World is not the product of political science or economic theory. It is not an arbitrary creation. Some of our national borders are arbitrary creations—legacies of colonialism—but the things we share as people are sustained by a common historical experience. It is this experience under a century or more of foreign domination that brings us together. From Asia, Africa, and Latin America; from the Caribbean and the Pacific; we confront the same problems, strive for similar goals, and share the conviction that we have much to gain by working together.

The leaders who met at Bandung thirty years ago recognised this and demonstrated their understanding of the value of solidarity. There was a desire to work together to find common solutions. In the past thirty years, the movement has grown; in the UN General Assembly, in UNCTAD, in the Group of 77, at Arusha, and in the North–South Dialogue. By the end of the 1970s, the Third World has coalesced into a political force. But this remains a very incomplete process. Summitry and conference diplomacy are one thing; building up the communications infrastructure and personal contacts necessary for real political development is another.

Although the UN Declaration on Decolonisation was passed by the General Assembly twenty-five years ago, the struggle continues. For the people of Namibia, Azania and Palestine, self-determination remains a dream. In the rest of the Third World, political independence has brought with it deception and disillusionment. Ruling elites have cynically relied on the colonial power structure; regretfully, many Third World leaders owe their office to a combination of brute force and the support of the old metropolitan powers. We cannot ignore this failure to break the colonial mould, both domestically and internationally.

You are all familiar with the distorted nature of the Third World economy. The trade patterns of the colonial era still prevail. Instead of trading with their neighbours, most Third World countries rely for the bulk of their trade on the North. It is not unusual for a product to begin as a raw material in one country, be shipped to the North for processing, and then return to a neighbouring country as a finished product. The same pattern holds true for the flow of information. News about the South is selected and processed in the North, while direct communication between the peoples of the Third World remains at a minimum. It is ironic that the nations of the South have been talking more to the North than to each other.

All the regions of the world are represented here today by our guest speakers, from the North as well as the regions of the South. We are here to learn from their experiences and perceptions. Let me just mention those which reflect the wide scope of our proposed deliberations.

We have from China Madame He Liliang who will point out to us the significance of her country's national revolution and the mammoth strides in the field of economic independence since 1949. Mr Michael Manley, former prime minister of Jamaica, one of the most authentic of Third World voices will talk about the present economic crisis and how it affects the life of the masses in the Third World. Mr Amir Jamal, a veteran nationalist from Tanzania, will reflect on the lessons of the decolonisation process in Africa. Señor Gabriel Valdes, a valiant and determined fighter for democracy and human rights, will acquaint us with his continuing experiences in Chile as well as assessing the impact of neocolonialism in South America. We will also have a myth-breaking contribution from Teresa Hayter discussing whether any reform of the World Bank is possible. Mr Altaf Gauhar, Editor-in-Chief of *South* magazine and Secretary-General of the Third World Foundation will reflect on the Asian experience.

Tomorrow, the second day of our deliberations, should give us an indication of how our friends from the North can help to get us out of a rut—the North–South dialogue deadlocked together with the threat of rising protectionism. I for one am looking forward to the prescription of Professor Emmerij of The Netherlands, the father of 'the basic needs' approach. We also have from Yugoslavia Professor Janez Stanovnik with his great experience of European and multilateral diplomacy who will point out whether there is a trend towards a new internationalism. And, finally, we have Austria's distinguished son and international statesman, Dr Bruno Kreisky, who I am sure will come up not only with a prescription to resuscitate the North–South dialogue but also identify viable projects that will make a lack of response to them very hard to understand.

While we set out to strike the balance-sheet of the decolonisation process, we all recognise that change, however slow, is taking place. There is a growing feeling that a new generation of leaders such as Prime Minister Mahathir of Malaysia, Prime Minister Rajiv Gandhi of India, President Alan Garcia of Peru and Prime Minister Robert Mugabe of Zimbabwe belong to a new breed of post-colonial leaders and are evolving a pragmatic approach to resolve the economic and political problems of their countries.

But regretfully, despite these beacons of hope there are many countries in the Third World that do not yet have popular and representative leadership. I hope that the deliberations of this seminar will reach the ears of a wider audience, and it is with these thoughts that I take this opportunity of welcoming you all.

2. Bruno Kreisky

Mr Federal Chancellor, Mr Minister, Ladies and Gentlemen, dear friends who have come from near and far!
I should like to welcome you most cordially on behalf of the Vienna Institute for Development. And to those of you who may not know this Institute too well I should like to say that this Institute will shortly celebrate an important anniversary. It was founded twenty-five years ago on the initiative of Pandit Jawaharlal Nehru, who was of the opinion that it should set itself the task of promoting cooperation between the industrialised countries and the newly-independent countries who were then beginning to be called the 'Third World'. Many other eminent persons assisted in the foundation of the Institute—which now has the honour of the title of the Vienna Institute for Development—and it has enjoyed international support from the beginning.

A primary and continuing purpose of the Institute has been to create and foster the climate and the conditions that are necessary to demonstrate the importance of such cooperative policies for all nations. In the course of the last twenty-five years it has become clear that even today there is more need for this work than we used to believe, more need for making people aware of the necessity to cooperate. At that time, the UN enjoyed great credibility and there were many new and important tasks which people felt the UN would be capable of resolving. In the intervening years our expectations have not been realised; although we realised that the tasks before the UN were tremendous and very difficult, we never felt at that time that things would come to what they are now. I am not going to say more about this now for I shall approach the subject in greater detail tomorrow.

Before I give the floor to the next speaker, I should like to pay tribute to one who passed away a short time ago, one of the co-founders of the Institute, our friend William Clark. Many of you may have known of him from his other activities, in particular his work as one of the Vice-Presidents of the World Bank. Indeed, we owe a great deal to him. He gave us a lot through his active cooperation. Again and again he successfully persuaded us to remain realists, to remain firmly grounded in reality. Let us pay tribute to him at this moment.

Introductory Statements

1. Fred Sinowatz

Mr Chairman, Bruno Kreisky, ladies and gentlemen

I am very, very glad indeed—and I would like to stress this—that I may welcome you to Vienna today. In my own name and on behalf of the Austrian Federal Government, I am particularly glad that so many renowned personalities from all parts of the world have followed Chancellor Kreisky's invitation to come to Vienna in order to discuss, as Dr Kreisky has said, one of the most central, most important and most difficult problems of our time. As one who has been fortunate enough to cooperate with him for a long time, I would like to thank Bruno Kreisky for sharpening our vision of these problems. At a very early stage he clarified them for us with a political imagination of a special nature, combined with great honesty and sincerity and the readiness to undertake concrete efforts.

As has already been hinted today, 1985 is characterised for us Austrians by a number of anniversaries, anniversaries which have been of great importance in our history, and also of great importance for our understanding of ourselves. The Federal Government has declared 1985 to be 'the year of contemporary history' in order to give it a special emphasis. This year marks, for example, the fortieth anniversary of the end of the Second World War and the beginning of the Second Republic, when modern Austria was reborn in its present form. It is also the thirtieth anniversary of the conclusion of the Austrian State Treaty, which after ten years of occupation by the Allied Forces gave us again independence, freedom and sovereignty and—what is particularly important—the unity of our country. It is also the thirtieth anniversary of our membership in the United Nations, which has given us an opportunity to cooperate actively with other countries in the international community of nations and to strengthen Austria's reputation as a useful and sincere member of that community.

But, ladies and gentlemen, at the same time, the government decided that this special year, this year of jubilees, should not be dedicated only to looking back and to reflection but that it has to be oriented towards the future. We wanted to open our eyes and those of others, to the years to come, and we wanted at the same time to define the role of Austria in the world.

Therefore, I am particularly glad that this meeting now calls to mind the twenty-fifth anniversary of the passing of the 'decolonisation resolution' of the UN. There can be no doubt that Resolution 1514 of the United Nations marks a true milestone. It initiated the process of peaceful decolonisation, one of the UN's greatest achievements. And this process has in fact changed the face of the world in a most fundamental way. When in 1955 Austria joined the UN, that organisation had little more than fifty members. At the present time there are 159. And most of these new members owe their freedom and sovereignty to that basic resolution.

Now, ladies and gentlemen, some of you may ask what a country like Austria which has never been a colonial power can contribute to a debate on decolonisation. There are a number of reasons why we can offer something here. On the one hand, we have had a highly concrete and painful experience with foreign occupation, foreign domination and with nationality problems in the course of our history. And there is such a thing as a collective historical memory. We have in our history been confronted by these problems, which are deeply rooted in our consciousness and which have greatly influenced our understanding and have indeed enhanced our understanding of these problems. And, secondly, I do believe that the very fact that we have no colonial past has enabled us to develop our relations with Third World countries on a different basis, on a basis of mutual confidence and understanding, not encumbered by inherited or current dependencies. Thirdly, and I would like to stress this particularly not only in my capacity as the Austrian Chancellor, but also as a social democrat. We introduce yet another element into this dialogue; the element of solidarity, solidarity with all those who are deprived of their most fundamental rights, solidarity with all those who live in misery, want and without hope for a better, for a brighter future.

I have already said that the process of decolonisation has decisively changed the face of the world, and there can be no doubt about it. The world of today, ladies and gentlemen, is no longer a world of the big powers; it is not in the hands only of the big powers. The world of today has become much more multifaceted and multilayered. The majority of humanity lives in the small countries of this globe and we, these small countries, cannot bring our military or economic power to bear in the international scene. But we can speak with all the moral weight and the weight of international solidarity and equality and equal rights for an international order in which the small countries too have their place and where they can develop in peace and security.

Today there are only very few countries and nations that suffer from foreign dominance and the days of colonialism are numbered. But colonialism appears in many different guises, in many different forms. Political domination by foreign countries may be drawing to a close, but new and perhaps even more enduring forms of dependence are coming to the fore and urgently require a solution.

Without any doubt, there is first of all the economic and financial dependency, a dependency in which so many countries of the Third World have been placed. We speak of the 'debt crisis', and this is a very bland and highly technical concept which can be appropriately introduced and employed in international meetings or in academic studies. But what is behind it? Behind it we find a terrible and most bitter form of dependence, where a state is no longer the master of its own economic development, and its people can no longer benefit as they should from the fruits of their labour. The situation in Ethiopia which we have witnessed recently has shaken the world, and yet we know that even as late as 1970 the African continent was self-sufficient as far as food supply was concerned. Natural disasters and antiquated forms of agricultural activity have led these countries into one of the most dreadful forms of dependence, namely, that they have to rely on assistance from outside for the survival of their people.

But there are also other forms of exploitation which are equally threatening. I should like to mention in particular the settlement in Third World countries of particularly harmful industries without any concern for the local environment. I have only touched upon a few of the great problems that exist, and there are many more. But all of them have one thing in common: no country will be able to solve these problems by its own efforts. In order to solve these problems policies have to be shaped through international cooperation, a cooperation of all the forces that we can master.

Security is not only a military matter. Security is a comprehensive complex, a pervasive desire of every individual and of every state aiming at the preservation of life in the widest sense of the term and a life worth living. And it is from the bottom of the heart that I say that this is also in particular the wish of our young people. It is in this spirit that I wish you every success for your deliberations.

2. *Peter Jankowitsch*

Federal Chancellor Sinowatz, Chancellor Kreisky, Distinguished Prime Ministers and Ministers, Your Excellencies, ladies and gentlemen

May I thank Chancellor Kreisky, founder and President of the Vienna

Institute as well as Mr Humayun Gauhar, the publisher of *South* magazine for the words of welcome they have just spoken and be allowed, at the outset of this important meeting—attended by such a highly distinguished audience— to describe, in a few words, not only the aims and purposes but perhaps also the ambition of this event.

This is of course first and foremost a conference on and about 'decolonisation', one of the profoundest, one of the most sweeping changes world history has brought to this century.

It is a conference about one of the great reversals of world history, decolonisation, that became the triumphant force replacing the world political order built by a handful of seafaring powers since the age of the great discoveries and completed at the turn of the nineteenth and twentieth centuries.

But it is also a conference about the forces that brought about this world historical phenomenon, forces that projected a revolutionary drive comparable only to the explosive energies emanating from the social movements born within the very same societies, the very same order that ultimately created the vast colonial empires of history.

It will be a conference about the triumphs, the finest hours, but also about some of the failures, the set-backs of a complex process that owes its existence not to a single factor, a single source, but that like all great historical movements appears as the unique blend and product of many political, economic, social and cultural ingredients.

Like its counterparts in the centres of the imperial, industrialised powers, decolonisation was first and foremost the brainchild of revolutionary and reformist thinkers, of visionaries and utopians.

All continents have contributed to the vision of a decolonised, a liberated Third World. In Africa, in the black communities of North America and the Caribbean, the vision of Pan-Africanism inspired great men like Dr du Bois, Marcus Garvey and David Price Mars.

It was in the conference halls of the Pan-Africanist movement in London, New York and Manchester that some of the most influential of the new leaders of Africa—Kwame Nkrumah, Jomo Kenyatta or Namdi Azikiwe—acquired political experience and attracted international attention.

It was in intellectual assemblies such as 'Présence Africaine' in Paris that young poets and writers like Leópold Sédar Senghor, Aimé Cesaire, Cheikh Anta Diop or Jacques Rabemananjara challenged the political and cultural foundations of colonialism.

But some of the most powerful ideas against colonial domination emerged from India where Mahatma Gandhi shook the foundation of British imperial power with the practice of non-violent resistance.

It is certainly true that colonialism and imperialism were not only challenged by ideas. Their foundations were severely shaken by two world wars and by the recurrent crises of its superstructure, the world economic system.

Thus the ramparts that were beginning to fall in the wake of the Second World War had already long since been undermined.

It must also be said in fairness that opposition to colonialism—today as yesterday—has always been a universal cause: the early opponents of colonialism were joined by German and Russian Social Democrats, by British Liberals and enlightened men and women of all continents and races.

It is because of these origins that decolonisation is not only synonymous with names like Kwame Nkrumah, Gamal Abdel Nasser and Jawaharlal Nehru but also such names as Fenner Brockway and Clement Attlee, Jean Rous and Pierre Mendes-France, and, at the other end of the political spectrum, Charles de Gaulle and Harold Macmillan.

We shall deal here, then, with a complex, a many-faceted, a fascinating phenomenon and the forces, as well as the values that have guided it. Because decolonisation has not only changed the physical, the geographical aspect of the world and brought more than 100 new sovereignties to the scene.

It has also added new concepts and values such as 'self-determination' to the universal code of ethics.

But this, I should like to add, is not only a conference about history, it is first and foremost a conference about the future.

While understanding of the past and of its lessons and analysis of the forces that have shaped the destinies of the Third World is essential to a grasp of the present we should, in the course of these two days, try to evaluate the future role of the emerging political and economic force that is the Third World decolonised.

That this is a question of uncommon importance results, first and foremost, from the simple fact that it concerns the fate of at least three-quarters of humanity.

But the future of the Third World is important also; it cannot be a matter of indifference, or—in the words of a leading neo-conservative—'benign neglect' because, today, in every conceivable way, the fates of North and South, of the Third and the two other worlds are linked together.

If today the Third World is not at peace, if, since the end of the Second World War, at least twenty million people have died in something like 140 or perhaps 150 wars, nearly all of them fought in the Third World; if then the Third World is not at peace, none of us will be at peace.

If today, major parts of the Third World live in poverty or near poverty, if economic growth in many Third World countries has ground to a halt and if many economies have experienced setbacks of unimaginable dimensions, world economic growth is threatened everywhere. Thus, whatever the scenarios for short-term, medium-term or long-term economic development in other parts of the world might be, the shadow of the Third World looms large over them.

It cannot therefore be a matter of indifference or benign neglect that, in the current, third development decade—according to recent UN estimates— Third World output in 1985 is projected at 5 per cent below the 1980 level, that, to speak of Africa alone, recession, desertification and drought have pushed back average income in sub-Saharan Africa to below the level achieved fifteen years ago and that the Third World debt—which might reach the staggering figure of 970 billion dollars by the end of the year—has forced at least seventy developing countries either into arrears or into debt rescheduling agreements.

These are only some of the reasons why the future of the Third World will hold the answer to the future of humanity as such. Many more will become apparent during the debates of the coming two days.

But it is safe to assert at even this early state of our deliberations that much as the rise of the superpowers in world politics, the unleashing of atomic energy and the opening up of outer space the appearance of the Third World promises to be one of the most significant and profoundest changes in this century.

Decolonisation has changed the world beyond recognition. There are now some 177 sovereign states, most of them members of the United Nations, and a few more are to come in the not too distant future: Namibia, New Caledonia or Micronesia, to name but a few.

Certainly not all expectations linked to the spectacular political rise of the Third World have been fulfilled.

Has the decolonised Third World become a new centre of political power? Has the decolonised Third World satisfied the enormous hopes of its people for increasing prosperity? Has the decolonised Third World assumed the high moral authority that its first leaders, Kwame Nkrumah, Julius K Nyerere, Leópold Senghor, and Jawaharlal Nehru have projected?

These are some of the questions to be answered over the next two days.

While no attempt shall be made here to pre-empt the combined wisdom and experience of many distinguished speakers as well as the contribution we expect from an equally distinguished Austrian and international audience, let me at least indicate the spirit that, I hope, will prevail in our debates.

Let me therefore express the hope that this might be an appropriate forum and a propitious moment to challenge some of the most current misperceptions about the Third World and its real contributions to the march of history.

Let me express the hope that we shall be able to do justice to its achievements but also to its aspiration and challenge, with objective facts and analyses, those who can only see political chaos and moral despair, challenge the prophets of doom who pretend that its high ideals, its moral authority has degenerated into dictatorships and tyranny, mismanagement and waste, its voice in the great world fora into a steam-rolling voting machine.

Learning from the history of decolonisation and evaluating in a just and objective fashion the role of its most tangible product, the Third World also holds important lessons for the present.

Decolonisation, the process of liquidation of the injustices and iniquities that were accompanying it is far from over, self-determination of nations remains a goal that lies at the heart of many of the conflicts that tear the contemporary Third World apart.

As the history of decolonisation shows there is but little hope to solve these conflicts—from the ghettos of Soweto to the mountains of Afghanistan, from the tribulations of the Palestinian people to the turmoil in Central America—unless some of the most elementary rights and freedoms can be bestowed on those that are today deprived of them. And as the history of decolonisation shows equally well there is no way back: freedom once dearly conquered will not be easily abandoned. Even though Third World peoples may be poor and badly governed, even though many material amenities may—temporarily—disappear with the colonial power, the ideal of freedom and independence has always proved to be stronger than any other motive, material or otherwise.

These may be ambitious aims and hopes.

Not all of them may be realised in the course of two short days. We believe, however, that something meaningful may come about if in the course of our debates some realistic assessments of the real potential of the Third World can be reached, some vision of the new kind of partnership and cooperation that its existence demands can emerge.

The Third World is not only an idea and a hope for its people, it is a reality with which we have to come to grips. To understand this reality, to adjust to its need may perhaps sooner than many of us believe, become an important prerequisite not only for our common good but for our common survival.

3. *Thorvald Stoltenberg*

Since I am invited to say a few introductory remarks I will use this opportunity to give some very brief remarks because since I have been a speaker now and then myself, I am always worried about the introductory remarks of the Chair because usually the Chair will take some of my points. So this is no sort of revenge. I will be very brief. But I would like to take this opportunity to refer to some of the obvious conclusions from yesterday's deliberations.

One is that charity is not enough in North–South relations. The kindness of the industrialised countries can be measured. There is one way in which we can measure kindness but it indicates that we are only kind to the extent of 0.35% of our Gross National Product. We have been varying from 0.11 per cent to 1 per cent with the average usually between 0.33 per cent and 0.35 per cent.

We agree that a realisation of 'common interest' is necessary. It is one thing to say 'the common interest' of North and South, but a quite different thing is to understand it, to feel it as a part of your daily life. It is not enough just to be able to give a good speech and explain intellectually how our long-term interests coincide. It is also necessary to be much more brutal with ourselves and see to what extent do the short term interests coincide—I say this because I see lots of politicians around this table and all politicians know that long-term interests are fine for parliamentary speeches but not for everyday decisions! So, we have also to seek short-term common interests. Let me briefly mention two.

One I would call the security aspect of the North–South relationship. I call it the 'security aspect' not only because I think it is a reality but also for didactic reasons. I have noticed, as have most of you, that when it comes to security issues everyone feels that this is an immediate day-to-day interest. I believe that the combination of the increasing frustrations felt in the Third World combined with easier access to nuclear weapons is probably one of the most immediate and dangerous security issues we are facing.

You will recall that in December 1983 the UN published a list of thirty-five (thirty-five!) new countries that were on the verge of either being able to produce nuclear weapons or may already have them. And I mention this because in many ways, I am more worried about the issues we are not dealing with daily than those we are concerned with. And when I say 'we'—now I talk as a Northerner—in the North we are constantly preoccupied with the East-West security issue. And this is right, of course, but it is of concern to me that we treat North–South relations and also the security aspect of these relations as less important or as charity work. This in my opinion increases the threat and the danger of the further development of this combination of frustrations and proliferation. Let me now mention the other short-term common interest.

We often meet in our own countries the following attitude: 'We understand that the North–South relationship is important and we understand the economic issues, but it is a pity that it comes to a head when we ourselves have so many problems in the industrialised countries: unemployment, economic problems.' I believe, personally, that if we make progress in North–South relationships—and we do have to make progress—then it is not in spite of our own problems, it is because of our own problems. I doubt if we had continued our economic progress onwards from the 1960s and the early 1970s, whether we then would have been able to take North–South issues more seriously, both in general and in economic terms. I believe that the recognition of the fact that the old economic instruments do not work effectively any longer makes us a bit more open for new openings, new ways of thinking about the North–South situation whilst attempting to solve the problems of the industrialised countries. So, these are to me the areas of immediate short-term common interest: security, economy, employment.

The contributions this morning will deal with exactly these issues. The first on North–South cooperation is entitled 'Turning the tide'. I must say I am pleased to see that title for surely we do have to turn the tide now. I will not introduce Bruno Kreisky; that would be a waste of time. But what I would like to do is to put a personal note to Bruno Kreisky. I must say, and I know I share this with lots of other people, that we have many, many times been very thankful for your ability to say the right thing at the right moment even if what you say is not fully understood by all the actors in the current political play. This is important for every one of us, it is an inspiration and it is the mark of leadership, international leadership which we need so much.

Decolonisation: what paths?

Michael Manley

It is a brave man who can maintain the confident optimism which attended the decolonisation process and its aftermath up to ten years ago. Today, we see the Third World in the grip of crisis. Its combined debt of well over 1,000 billion dollars staggers the imagination, strangles national economies and frustrates hopes. Massive repayment schedules are draining foreign exchange, robbing the economic process of its vital sustenance as surely as if the blood supply were starved of oxygen.

Confident calls for a new international economic order which occupied a significant place in the world agenda during the 1970s have given way to a scramble for survival as the tactics of crisis management replace strategies of development. Deflationary adjustment policies have placed democratic gains in Latin America under siege while sub-Saharan Africa struggles with famine, as chronic malnutrition there gives way to starvation.

To understand the present crisis one has to look at the two sets of factors. Firstly, and most importantly, one has to look at the world economy, developments within it and their effect upon the Third World. Secondly, one has to consider developments within the Third World itself granted its particular place within the world economy.

As always, we must remind ourselves that the central dilemma of the Third World begins with its location within the world economy as a consequence of that cruel division of labour which was both the purpose and the result of widespread colonialism from the beginning of the sixteenth century. By condemning part of the globe to the production of commodities for the industrial revolution, modern imperialism created that two-headed monster, 'structural dependence' and 'chronic under-development'.

Inevitably, economic strategies following political independence, wherever this has taken place, have been concerned with industrialisation and diversification of agriculture. In both cases, simple import substitution appeared to be the necessary path to change and development. However, experience soon showed that efforts to expand local food production along with the new factories which were producing consumer goods for the home markets were not a final answer, but, at best, only a beginning. For example, production for home consumption involved imported inputs such as fertilisers and insecticides. The new factories would have to import the raw materials, probably energy also and, almost certainly, machinery and spare parts. In a sense, therefore, for any new factory to make garments far from decreasing structural dependence would only diversify it. At the same time, the process would increase the dependence of a particular economy on foreign exchange. In earlier times one might have responded to a shortage of foreign exchange by reducing imports of certain kinds of clothing. In the new situation, garment sales could represent investment and jobs in a factory. Hence it would no longer be feasible to contemplate saving foreign exchange by suspending the importation of inputs such as cloth, buttons, thread and spare parts because major social dislocation would be involved.

None of this is said by way of criticism because, as with all processes of change, economic development is a learning experience. By the beginning of the 1970s Third World development thinkers were getting to grips with the complexities that beset economic expansion and diversification. 'Basic needs' strategies were formulated. The necessity to plan forward and backward linkages, so as to utilise local raw materials and to investigate by-product opportunities was coming to be understood. The Third World was realising that it was not enough to get in at the tail-end of the first world economic process. One also had to retrace the steps of history to see what other stages of the economic process could be relocated at home.

Even as new understandings reflected growing maturity, other developments were taking place in the world economy. Some were of historic significance. The chronically adverse terms of trade ensured that Third World commodities declined in purchasing power against capital goods. The effort at diversification, therefore, was being attempted in a context where capital accumulation had to contend with the drain in wealth produced by the terms of trade even while the rising expectations of historically-deprived people exerted their separate pressure upon resources.

And then came the Vietnam War. The over-supply of money triggered the surge in grain and other prices of goods trading in the world economy. In due course, the OPEC countries reacted with rises in the price of oil and so the stage was set for that gross aggravation of a chronic condition which came to be known as 'stagflation'. Overnight, Third World governments found the traditional inputs upon which their economies depended priced out of reach. In the meantime, incomes were falling as commodity markets contracted. To other disadvantages was now added the crisis of foreign exchange.

One need not recount in detail the agony that was to follow the events of 1973. For most Third World economies, borrowing was not an indulgence but the only means to survival. It was not a question of mismanagement and incompetence encouraged by dreams of grandeur. Largely, it was a situation where countries were struggling to survive—a situation where drugs were lacking in hospitals and plant in factories. As the problem of survival grew more acute in the next ten years so did the rise in the price of survival, twelve-year money became eight and then five; and eight per cent interest rates became ten and twelve and even fourteen per cent. Thus, just at the very moment that Third World economic planners were developing a sophisticated understanding of what was needed to be done, solutions became increasingly a pipe dream for money was no longer a means to development. Borrowed money became, first, a means to survival; then, because of its cost, money became a new cause of disaster.

We must, perhaps, pause here to retrace our steps and look at the other part of the equation. Throughout the 1960s the growing understanding of the internal economics of development had its parallel in a better grasp of the world economy and how it works. Hence, the Third World began to fashion a set of specific proposals for a better and more equitable management of the world economy. I have sometimes wondered if the term 'New International Economic Order' (NIEO) does not conceal rather than illuminate reality. It has a rhetorical flourish which suggests that the world economy is about to be re-designed and relocated on Mars. On the contrary, the NIEO consists of a set of realistic and eminently practical adjustments and adaptations to ensure that the world economy is more rationally managed and that its management shall be directed to sensible and equitable ends. Even as the free-marketeers seek to perpetuate the myth of a free international market, Third World thinkers were beginning to grasp the extent to which the multinational corporation system has abolished the free market. These corporations have increasingly gained control over the majority of world trade and substituted their own centrally-planned determination of which factors of production to exploit and where, which transfer prices to apply, and which mix of the two will make the most profits.

In the face of the new reality, the arguments for a common fund—for modifying the decision-making process of the International Monetary Fund (IMF) and providing the means for a developmental perspective rather than an adjustmental perspective in its operations—these are not an invasion of some happy, idyllic free market as contemplated by Adam Smith. Instead, they represented and still represent an attempt to create an environment that is more favourable to the prospect of Third World development. And to the extent that Third World development was facilitated the first world itself would be a permanent beneficiary from the enlarged world economy that would result. Another canard that must be scotched is that Third World countries fight against IMF 'conditionality' because the Fund insists on efficient management. The truth is that it is resisted because it crushes developing countries into short-term adjustments with which they are ill-equipped to cope.

All of this has now gone by the board. Forward and backward linkages and by-product utilisation represent economic strategies which are logical extensions of the imperative of import substitution. In its turn, import substitution is the necessary precursor to a relocation of Third World economies in the international division of labour. The NIEO represents an attempt to provide a framework of equitable opportunity within which the strategies of internal economic transformation may be pursued. As we remarked earlier, crisis is the order of the day and survival is the first order of business. Even as the shortage of foreign exchange was creating the debt crisis, changes of significance were occurring in the political system of the first world, where there had been thirty years of change and expansion of the 'welfare state' seemingly based on advancing technology and expanding demand. These were the foundations visible to the naked eye. Hidden, but essential to this process, however, was the assured supply of low-priced inputs in the shape of energy and commodities from the Third World. When the post-Vietnam contradictions were countered by OPEC, the end of an era was signalled. The long noontime between 1945 and 1975 was replaced by a broken twilight when contraction and inflation co-existed to produce stagflation, the stage was set for Friedman, monetarism, supply-side economics, Reagan, Thatcher and the re-emergence of the radical Right as the dominant force in first world politics and ideology.

The people-oriented economics of the post-war era in Europe represented a time when the interests of the majority dominated the political agenda. Then the minority at the pinnacle of the system struck back with a vengeance. The North–South dialogue became a monologue as Third World voices retreated in silence with yet another balance-of-payments crisis. In the meantime, the new US administration lectured the rest of us about the virtues of a system long since past and which they have no intention of reinstating. For Third World planners it is now clear, for the time being at least, that the way forward is not likely to have the benefit of a more favourable environment.

The law of the sea has been effectively scuttled. The Common Fund plan languishes on the shelves of UNCTAD. The IMF is presiding over one social disaster after another, its current prescriptions inevitably guaranteeing the contraction of those poorer parts of the world economy that most desperately need to expand. The economics of deflation hold Europe in a state of suspended animation with unemployment nearing thirty million. The contracting effects of 'beggar my neighbour' demand-management disrupts the normal patterns of Third World development. The IMF prescription erodes the foundations of home markets and ensures that home populations grow increasingly hungry and ill-clad as Third World economies are twisted, distorted and warped in the pursuit of the mirage of export surpluses which they have not the means to earn. It is a sad, sorry, dismal and sick picture of misconceived remedies in which the victims are blamed. Inappropriate medicines are forced down the throats of patients who will soon be brought by foolish care to a condition where they will have to be transferred from the general wards for the sick to the intensive care units for the terminally ill.

What is the way forward? One is tempted to ask: Is there a way forward? I believe that there is, partly because I have to so believe, partly because this is not the first crisis in the history of a civilisation which is increasingly global in character and interdependent, and partly because there are responses to which the Third World is challenged by its circumstances. Let us assume that the basic economic environment is going to remain hostile for the next few years; if so, certain issues must be addressed.

Firstly, we need a more complete understanding of the nature of the development process itself. A nation is developed to the extent that it can formulate worthwhile objectives for itself; that it can achieve an effective consensus about those objectives; that it can optimise the use of its own resources in the attainment of those objectives; that it can educate and train its people so that their capacities are relevant to those objectives; and that it can achieve the levels of will, energy, consistency and stamina without which the objectives will become rhetorical proclamations rather than the focus for effort. Development, therefore, is the sum total of the political, social and economic capacities of a society and the way in which each interacts positively with the rest. This clearly implies a process that must begin within the political system, for it is here alone that objectives can be defined, analysed, debated and determined. At the same time, levels of social development as measured by the range and quality of education or the state of health, will themselves affect both the process and the outcome of the search for consensus; so too will they affect economic activity and the institutions through which all of these are regulated and articulated. Hence, development planning must begin within the political process, but must also take account of the interaction of economic and social factors.

Perhaps the greatest challenge of all today is to be found in the need for Third World countries to re-examine their political processes in order to ensure that they provide the opportunities for widespread and effective democratic participation. It is only when people have the opportunity to participate and communicate at the community, the regional and the national level within and through appropriate institutions that one can hope to achieve consensus; such a process of building consensus will ensure a realistic balance of aspirations and possibilities. If goals are set within a time-frame of expectations that bears no relation to reality, then the goals themselves will become a source of frustration and eventual despair. Political debate, therefore, must not shrink from exposing all the harshest realities to all the people all of the time.

All of this is a roundabout way of distinguishing 'the politics of mobilisation' from 'the politics of expectations'. If the people are not involved in the political process, they cannot be expected to contribute to the outcome. On the other hand, if the political process itself conceals the nature of struggle behind meaningless promises then despair can be the only outcome.

The implications of all this can, perhaps, best be illustrated by reference to the great unexplored opportunity of the South which is cooperation between its members. 'South–South' remains a part of the rhetorical agenda as distinct from the strategic agenda for two reasons. In the face of present crisis, governments lack the capacity to pursue strategies that are necessarily long-term. Conditions make this bad enough, but there is a deeper cause of this ailment. This is to be found in the nature of 'South–South' cooperation on the one hand and the quality of the political process on the other. There is no statement of intent for the Third World that lends itself more readily to rhetoric and less easily to action than 'South–South cooperation'. It is a task that involves long, hard practical planning of how factors of production may be developed and combined to create incremental economic capacity. It is to do with how to de-link certain, not all, elements of the economy of the South from the North as part of the process of structural transformation and in answer to the crisis of structural dependence. But whether it be two South–South countries combining to produce a new food complex, or a new shipping line or new patterns of trade, a mastery of the subtleties of opportunity cost analysis is required. Cadres which have been employed in the management of crisis must be transferred to the tasks of positive planning. Exemplary and unprecedented levels of will, determination, clarity of purpose and dedication are required. Strategies which are built upon coordinated specific targets must be evolved. About ten years ago there was a good example of a missed opportunity for South–South cooperation. The creation of a Caribbean food corporation was suggested at a moment when world crises threatened to cripple Caribbean governments.

So much for the demands upon governments. But what are the demands upon people? Where political consciousness operates within the time-span of the immediate, there is often no patience with that longer time-span which is a necessary part of strategic planning. For example, it may take ten years from the time when three Third World countries decide to pool their individual resources of energy, raw materials and market in order to create a new aluminium industrial complex. Foreign inputs will be necessary, but if it is to be an effective exercise, part of the enterprise must come from internal capital formation. Where will the patience and endurance come from to make this possible?

It is no longer a part of the practical political prospectus to assume that capital accumulation can be accomplished (as in the nineteenth century) by the crude exploitation of the working classes. Therefore, the political process must attend to questions of relative equity within society so that the system provides incentives. However, the disparities must not become so great as to make mobilisation impossible. This problem must first be resolved within the political process before one can move to the next and overwhelmingly necessary second stage of planning and implementation.

Ironically, there is no area of the current dilemma more replete with possibilities for disaster or progress than that question of debt with which we began with this discussion. As long as it persists—the source of an unending haemorrhage of foreign exchange—everything else is a mockery. Yet the answer to this crisis lies partly in the hands of the Third World itself. There has never been a more dramatic opportunity to demonstrate the only semi-jesting, Keynesian analysis of the shift in power that occurs from creditor to debtor as debt itself grows. Led by the Latin American debtor nations, the Third World has the capacity to use the debt itself as the means to force an international conference to discuss the resolution of the crisis by the reorganisation and rescheduling of the burden. The problem here is that the Third World will not combine in the arena of action; indeed, it can hardly summon the will to combine in the arena of rhetoric.

The Cartagena Conference of Debtor Countries at the beginning of 1985 set out a practical plan for re-structuring and re-ordering world debt. This has been adopted by the bureau of the Socialist International and endorsed by no less a voice than that of Willy Brandt. The plan calls for a massive rescheduling of part of the debt, possibly including a bond issue, underwritten by creditor countries. Specifically, this would enable the cancellation of the debt of the least developed countries; in particular, the debt of sub-Saharan Africa, for their proportion of the total is small and their capacity to repay virtually non-existent. Thereafter, a massive re-scheduling exercise could begin with a moratorium and incorporate two principles; firstly, that no country would be obliged to repay past debt at more than a given percentage of its foreign exchange earnings (we propose twenty per cent); and, secondly, that there be a cap on interest rates so as to prevent that element in the equation from undermining the intentions implicit in the rest of the exercise.

If the Third World could come together to demand and compel the holding of a debtor-creditor conference—which it is in their capacity to do—they would at a stroke give a practical demonstration of South-South cooperation leading to changes in the fundamental condition which they all face, by which they are currently paralysed and which unresolved is a block to all future progress. Such a conference could be required to look at some of the structural problems and, in particular, the reorganisation of the World Bank and the IMF in respect of decision-making, lending capacity and basic policy.

This is but one example of what we need to do. If we could find a way to do it, doors might open in our own minds that lead on to other projects, other ventures and a general resumption of forward momentum. At the same time, we must act to create a long-overdue Third World Secretariat. This could incorporate the informal start already made at the UN by some members of the group of 77. It could service both the group of 77 and the Non-Aligned Movement, and could be formally attached to either. It could develop an agenda for a conference on debt, examine the feasibility of South-South projects, sharpen Third World negotiating skills; in short, maintain forward momentum by showing where each practical forward step could be taken with assurance and growing confidence!

Viewing the options

Amir Jamal

Mr Chairman

I feel deeply honoured to have been given this invaluably privileged opportunity to speak in Vienna this morning under the joint auspices of the Vienna Institute of Development and *South*, the Third World magazine.

The Vienna Institute under the inspired guidance of Chancellor Bruno Kreisky is indeed a vintage institution, something which perhaps comes naturally to Vienna and Austria. *South* magazine has been maturing and mellowing at a pace at which its many friends find good reason in rejoicing, even as it continues to replenish itself with new approaches and endeavours to give voice to the South.

Having spoken more than a few times on the subject of decolonisation, there is a danger of repeating many things, perhaps several times over. I must plead guilty in advance.

I shall take certain things as granted. There is no point in rediscovering the wheel, so to speak, though in the condition of present-day Africa, the wheel is in much greater demand than can be met in time to meet the needs of many million human beings.

I must assume that statistics about Africa, in so far as they have validity, are available to all serious-minded observers and students of contemporary African history. Those who have the time and the inclination will find that comparison of current statistics about literacy, manpower development and state of health, no less than those about bureaucracies and defence establishments with those of 25 years ago, are of some value in judging both the potential of what can be achieved and the prospects of what can only be described as further retrogression of an already acutely difficult situation.

Also I shall not bemoan the stark fact that Africa is a grievously fragmented continent, comprising a range of countries of sizes and endowment, natural geographical and historical, a fact which will continue to determine the future course of history. At the same time, there is no case for showing helplessness in the matter of a very high rate of population increase.

As for what decolonisation has done and is doing to the colonisers themselves—to their psychology, to their structures, to the reformulation of their national interests—it is perhaps a subject for another seminar, if such a need is felt by those concerned.

It is often said that the nation-state is a Eurasian concept. European and Asian history is seen to illustrate, indeed to justify this view. Over the centuries, hordes of soldiers under the command of war-lords crossed, back and forth, boundaries of areas that were being settled by pastoral societies, remaining in occupation sometimes for a short duration, at other times over a longer time-span running even into centuries, as was the case with the Ottoman Empire. With the passage of time, political borders became more defined, though subject to the shifting of relative power from decade to decade. So, when the Europeans imposed boundaries on Africa in 1885, they were treating their respective colonial interests in Africa in the same mould as they had become historically used to doing with regard to their own interests nearer home, imposing borders on one another in accordance with the then prevailing relative strength. The only difference—it was of course fundamental—was that they treated Africa as their territory.

The two World Wars were, in historical terms, a continuation of the same process, although the organic reality of European geography and culture on the one hand, and trade and exchange arising from the interaction of these contiguous societies and above all the imperialist elements and forces within them on the other hand, extended the area of conflict to a much larger portion of the globe.

While everything else was thrown into the melting-pot of history to emerge again within political boundaries, old and new (which as I have already said was the continuation of a now familiar process) Africa's political boundaries became frozen by the very logic of the offspring of imperialism devoutly wishing not to open up a Pandora's Box, by attempting to redefine those boundaries. Incalculable damage would result to the prospects of developing unity on the basis of stability and prosperity of each political entity, which was the perceived objective of independent African countries finally to be enshrined in the OAU Charter itself.

The lowering of the imperial flag and the raising of national flags signalled but the beginning of a historically involuted process. Immediately, almost instantly, a typical African state was expected to spin out an outer shell, marked on the map by its political boundaries, diverting the bulk of its meagre economic and social resources to building up all the accoutrements of sovereignty such as a Head of State, a Council of Ministers, a government administration, diplomatic representation, membership of the UN and other international organisations; not to mention the ministries of External Affairs, Internal Affairs and of Defence to contend with the floodgate of influences that were to impinge on the newly-born political entity that must now forge itself into a sovereign nation. You have to imagine the hypothecation of resources—training of manpower, provision of urban amenities such as water, electricity, roads, and drainage, telephones, housing equipment of various descriptions to suit the needs of ministries and ministers—to realise the disproportionately heavy price for what was supposed to be the beginning of the process of decolonisation. The irony of it all was the accentuation of the very colonial system of education, the urgency with which it had to be accelerated to enable the manning of the administrative apparatus, teachers had to be drawn from the same colonial sources to train teachers to produce teachers to teach students. There was no early escape from having to strengthen the very colonial structures which had kept colonial rule going.

If one then superimposes on it all the anatomy of the economy that was already in place, primary, export market-dependent production to be exchanged with products of industrial technology with its price-setting categorical imperative, the struggle of an escape from the colonial/imperial scheme of things could only have been sustained by sheer political organisation and political will.

If the process of decolonisation is to be judged by the manner in which the inherited structures have been recast, reorganised, or even discarded and replaced within the national boundaries of each sovereign African country, the question which history must answer in due course is whether those who succeeded in making that process deliberate and measured have gained sufficient time for African societies to want to resist the dismantling of those structures through arbitrary authoritarianism in favour of an orderly democratic process of evolution as a means to that end.

The path of decolonisation is not unlike a field strewn with land-mines, exploding in the face of leadership as society inches forward, putting in place socio-economic structures responsive to its own perceived needs. It is hardly surprising that in so many cases, the direction seems to have been lost in the debris resulting from explosions along the way and sometimes even despair taking hold of the national psyche.

If there is surprise it is in the fact that so many national exertions have survived these enormous obstacles under leadership capable of steering the ship—to alter the analogy—through stormy, uncharted seas, and to provide grounds for hope of an effective self-fulfilling future.

As is to be expected, the pre-independence colonial period was itself one of struggle on the part of the indigenous societies on three main fronts, all at the same time. There was the time-worn struggle against the elements, the weather, the wild animals and pests, the harsh soil conditions, waged with primitive technology which itself had been the product of trial and error spanning over centuries. Then came the struggle of having to contend with the intrusion of the foreigner. Totally alien, with no easy way of communicating on any agreed wavelength, this made the traditional task of survival even more intractable. And the abrasive chemistry of interaction between native and alien values created a whole new set of problems particularly for the younger, growing section of the community, whose process of self-development had so far been contained in the overall evolution of a socially balanced community, which now found itself churned up and thrown into the melting-pot fuelled by incomprehensible alien action and predictable native reaction.

Goran Hyden is not the only chronicler of Tanzania's experience—from the pre-colonial times through colonial history and into the post-independence period of striving for social equilibrium—who has perceived the inherent strength of the peasant community to survive in the face of all these odds. The contribution of Hyden and others is of value, especially because it is a recurring reminder to the urban-centred post-independence national leadership that the chances of failing to retain organic links of meaningful communications with the vast peasantry are much greater than is generally believed; that at the very least, the peasantry should not be taken for granted and that much more deliberate 'decolonisation' of the urban mind is called for without much delay.

The dilemma that the new post-independence leadership faces is both very real and, in its essence, quite cruel. In my view, Hyden does not give adequate recognition and appreciation of the objective elements historically embedded in the soil of Africa's—certainly Tanzania's—political economy. It is one thing to observe, quite correctly, that 'it can be said that the German colonisation of Tanganyika effectively put an end to the prosperity of the indigenious pre-colonial economies', or to assert, again quite correctly that 'the British revealed *their* narrow understanding of the African peasant economy', at the very beginning of this century. It is quite another thing to have to contend *today* with the consequences of those failures, as the post-independence leadership must do, having itself been the product of a system which was built on that historical ignorance of the peasantry. That the post-independence leadership did not create the system which produced it is now irrelevant except as a matter of historical record. However, the system which created the intellectual content of the new, urban-centred leadership, far from disappearing became more intensively accentuated even as it was being adapted in order to contend with both the external environment and the internal reality represented by the vast peasantry, which in the final event is the producer of the economic goods.

For those who may be interested in the impact of a pervasively decisive aspect of the external environment on the indigenous process, I have requested the Institute to make available a copy of my intervention at a conference organised by the Social Democratic Party of the Federal Republic of Germany, eight years ago.

The process of decolonisation, seen this way, has to be the decolonisation of the mind itself. Only then, at every turn of the screw by the relentlessly impinging external environment, would it be possible for the new leadership to perceive the options in terms of whether they imply slightly less rather than more reliance on the external forces. And while it would be unscientific to say that extending the area of dependence on the external influences and resources automatically implies a further alienation of the peasantry, the chances must be rated as very high of continuing to be pre-empted into a trajectory, which places an enormous strain on the as yet fragile organic links between the urban 'colonised' mind and the rural uncontaminated peasantry.

Any conceptualisation of the decolonisation process which emphasises only the importance of disengagement from the inherited tracks laid down by the colonial system would, and I believe should, be criticised as being of negative value. In this inter-locked world, the process of linking with the rest of the world is inevitable, even if it had not already in many respects been pre-determined.

How do we reduce our dependence on the external world even in an area where we are clearly at the mercy of the so-called 'magic' of the market? The more coffee the coffee-growers of the world produce the more certain is the collapse of the price structure, which at the best of times is precariously fragile. Precisely the same is true of sugar and tea and several other primary products. Do we uproot the trees, the bushes and the plants? How can the clock be put back on all the social, physical and political infrastructure, on the soldiers and the schools and the universities, the service workers and the administrators? Will the peasantry be left to its own subsistence devices when the linkages with the urban centres are not only physical in the form of roads and telephones and transport services, but more importantly through kith and kin, are of political significance in all the spheres I have enumerated and more?

If criticism has to be levied on the new leadership in the post-independence period, it is in the failure on its part to perceive in time the importance of choosing priorities, not only priority in terms of the goals but perhaps of much more decisive significance, priority in terms of means to be deployed.

Considering the absence of any experience in planning and managing a national economy, the failure to perceive the relevance of options was altogether understandable. A single economist or a group of economists may be trained in a period of a few years after completing university education to comprehend the significance, in theory, of putting in place a compatible package of macro-economic policy instruments, consistent with perceived socio-economic objectives. But without this understanding being transposed to the entire democratic process of decision-making and perhaps of even greater relevance, without having the institutional framework and critical mass of resources to enable macro-economic management to be delivered to the field at the micro level it was wholly predictable that the majority of the African countries would have to go through a particularly trying period. If the 1960s were a relatively tranquil period, it was because it was characterised by a number of coincidences. The lessons of the World War were still fresh in the minds of industrialised societies, leading to the instituting of the Bretton Woods systems for the regulation of international economic relations. There was the inevitable period of inertia on the part of the developing countries emerging from a colonial experience, structure and status. There was leadership in the industrialised societies consciously looking for policy elements to be put in place in order to enable social and political balance to be established in international affairs, through the instrumentality of the UN system. The 1970s and the 1980s have, on the other hand, witnessed the abandonment of internationalism in all its material and spiritual aspects and the jettisoning of the fragile, incipient African economies on to the shifting quicksands of power-manipulated market operations.

All this has thrown into sharp relief the folly or perhaps error on the part of the new African leadership to assume that techniques of planning an economy could be deployed without being in a position to meet the necessary preconditions. It was never a question of deliberately not choosing priorities. The challenge was of putting the goal of manpower development, of relevance to a peasant society, at the top of the agenda. Not just training of university graduates, but embarking on an entire range of training of skills at various levels and of various specialisations; not an easy task at the best of times. It was a much more difficult first choice to make with the field still virgin in which to learn 'on-the-job'. It was literally having to break new ground and developing one's own yardstick with which to measure the validity of the choice and of the directions itself, even as the terms of reference of the global environment kept changing due to factors totally beyond the control of the new leadership.

The tragedy of our times is not that the newly-independent countries had not embarked on an inevitable process of developing their yardsticks arising from their 'on-the-job' experience. The tragedy is that this process in the case of most African countries received a serious jolt in the 1970s due to what can already be described as a reversal of the rules and policies which had steadily come into force in the wake of the Bretton Woods system. The logic of the system pointed towards a further evolution of the world's monetary and trade system to enable developing countries to take their place as active partners in the global process of trade and exchange through development. There were already so many weaknesses in that system due to the historical fact that the Bretton Woods system was itself predicated on the norms which were valid for market-oriented industrialised countries. Nevertheless, with political will, the system was capable of steady modification. Instead, increasingly it is the superior market power which has been dominating the global economic environment, with the less developed African countries becoming even more marginalised than before.

In the 1960s it seemed possible for the African countries to develop at a steady rate in economic terms while at the same time building their social infrastructure, by means of educational and training programmes. However, the world-wide inflation in the industrialised countries, combined with the major oil price shocks in the 1970s coinciding with the abandonment of the fixed exchange rate regime, the emasculation of IDA and the terms of trade of primary products turning severely adverse, little room was left for these struggling economies to take corrective action of the kind that any normal management of a national economy requires from time to time. When the soil is wet and muddy and a vehicle moving at normal speed gets its wheels stuck in it, more often than not, the engine running under its normal power even at the lowest gear only succeeds in making the wheels sink deeper in the mud. Such is the negative multiplier effect of cumulative loss of economic strength due to the factors about which international memory seems all too short.

The cruel irony of the situation is that the years of effort in training their own manpower in various sectors of the economy is already yielding most gratifying results in many African countries. Young engineers, scientists, managers, accountants and research workers are already grappling with down-to-earth problems, trying to make do with the simplest of equipment available in order to keep the economy on the move. Rejected pieces of steel, worn-out railway lines, second-hand tyres, and scores of other articles which in the industrialised societies have already found their way to the rubbish dumps, are becoming transformed into ox-carts, agricultural implements, pipes to convey water, machines to thresh maize and rice, and so on. Just six days ago, I spent a day in a rural development centre in Tanzania with a group of young, keen engineers and technicians who had completed two prototypes on the drawing board, and three others in the workshop, only to confront, helplessly, the bottleneck of transport without which it would not be possible to reach the village communities waiting to find some practical answers to their all-too-familiar problems.

The theme of this seminar is 'The Future of the Third World'. The future of course takes shape out of the present, very much as the present has taken shape out of the past. Two things can be stated with total conviction. One, the Third World will refuse to die. It will live and it will take its place in the global order. Two, the values which the Third World will want to see sustained in global relations are being conditioned by what has been happening in the late 1970s and what threatens to dominate the environment in the rest of the 1980s. The message of the environment is quite clear:

> We the wealthy, the possessors of capital and technology are feeling poor. Do not expect us to do anything about the global system which, it is just your bad luck, may be operating to your disadvantage. Maybe when we begin to earn sufficient wealth once again on a sustained basis, you will benefit from the spill-over. In the meantime do the best you can to adjust yourselves to this reality.

Obviously, with practically no room between the back and the wall, and the determination to survive, we may have reached a critical point where options never wide, are becoming narrower still while at the same time being more sharply defined.

Internally, the option between a conscious effort to root democracy in the soil on the one hand, and authoritarianism on the other hand may become increasingly an academic issue. Even where the democratic process had been severely damaged and the military option had been exercised, hope has continued to be cherished that at some point in time the process of rooting democracy in the soil would be restored. Once that hope is abandoned in the majority of African countries, the burden of keeping the flame burning will fall on even fewer societies than now.

On any realistic view of the world economy, with so many contending interests interacting with one another, there is either a rational internationally agreed framework in which institutions and policies mutually reinforce one another in the interest of balanced and sustained development, or a total failure of the system leads to the prevalence of the law of the jungle. What this means is that, somewhere down this road, there has to begin yet another round of determined effort to build a new order on the rubble of a world economy that collapsed, because it went out of anyone's control.

The Third World, including Africa, has no interest in any such collapse. What it can do to avoid such a state of affairs, without timely and adequate effort on the part of industrialised countries to place the larger and more dependable interests of the international community ahead of their own purely national self-interest, will depend on the quality and strength of leadership which the Third World countries can provide in their respective regions, as they make a conscious choice among very few and narrow options.

There never was any alternative to greater and more sustained effort at regional cooperation and integration in the socio-economic and political field. But now, more than ever, that way lies not only the survival of each of the constituent national entities but also the hope of contributing to the process of building global equilibrium. The Lagos Plan of Action, based on continental promotion of regional operations, calls for a closer understanding of the parts of the international community. While the early stages of such concerted effort is bound to be a most exacting task, once a framework is established for cooperation in a critical number of agreed areas, a snow-balling effect can take the process to a point where South–South cooperation becomes a global force which will have to be taken into account in any global compact. In an historical time-scale, with information technology accelerating at a pace that was unthinkable only a few years ago, such a prospect is not all that far away. Even in a least developed country such as Tanzania, carefully planned manpower development with unusual foresight, has in less than one generation produced an increasing reservoir of experienced administrators, managers, engineers, and scientists, not to mention trainers and teachers. Taking Africa as a group and adding its strength to the rest of the Third World, there is absolutely no field of human activity that cannot be undertaken in the larger interest.

Those in the Third World who, more than once, have been heard to say that it may not be all that against the interest of the developing countries, for the screw of international alignment of economic forces to be tightened just enough to compel them to close their ranks, may be right after all, especially if the alternative is extinction as self-respecting societies. Indeed for Africa, paradoxically because it was the latecomer on the contemporary world economic scene, with the debt of sub-Saharan Africa being much more burdensome relative to national wealth or annual rate of gross product, the choice may become brutally simple.

The more likely scenario, taking all factors into account, is that of some packaged international deal short of fundamental global reform, yielding enough time to relapse into a continuing state of dependence on the industrialised countries, on the basis of a combination of self-interest and charity. The hope must be that in such an event, the time thus made available will be seized with calculated determination to move even more rapidly in the direction of South–South cooperation and integration.

That this particular journey offers the best prospect to small and medium-sized industrialised countries to link themselves resolutely with such a process in their own longer term interest, may or may not be obvious to their present-day national leadership. It would have to be part of active policy-making of the developing countries themselves to include such a prospect deliberately in their agenda, also in their own long-term interest.

To give only one example. I have little doubt about the wisdom of extending railway systems and building new ones in Africa. The cost-benefits of a well-run railway system altogether outweigh those of road transport systems by a wide margin. Besides, railways form a more lasting link between contiguously placed countries, and provide a sound infrastructural framework for a food security regime on a regional basis. The longer Africa takes to become disillusioned with the glossiness of the road transport system, other than as a feeder to a trunk system of railways, the costlier and slower is going to be the attainment of the goal of sustained self-reliance. Africa needs to have a common basic perception in respect of a number of key policy areas including monetary harmonisation in which concerted action could begin immediately, with the active involvement of a number of small and medium-sized industrialised countries.

Let me conclude by saying that there are two options for moving towards a global equilibrium. One is on the basis of the rest of the world being grouped into two satellite camps, one belonging to each superpower. We may laugh at such a prospect today. But overwhelming military superiority sustained by an enormous industrial complex has its own logic, even if in the end, like the dinosaur it ends up on the scrap-heap of history. The other one, the rational and altogether fulfilling option is of developing countries, in close collaboration with small and medium-sized industrial societies, to begin the crucially important task of laying the foundations of a stabilising process of the equitable distribution of power stemming from economic strength that is dedicated to the attainment of fair play, social justice and prosperity for the greatest number. Prosperity pre-empted by a few offers no promise of global equilibrium, only of global despair.

Latin America: neocolonialism and democratisation

Gabriel Valdes

The Latin American political scenario

Colonisation and its consequences

Throughout the three centuries of colonial dependence on Spain (1492–1810), apart from Cuba, which was liberated eighty years later, Latin America was broken up into 'Viceroyalties' and 'Captaincies-General' which were completely isolated from each other and all directly dependent on a Spanish state body. This dependency ruled out any commercial or political link between the colonies. This reality has left deep marks on Latin American international relations which remain up to the present day.

Independence was a collective political phenomenon, drawing inspiration from the Anglo-American and French revolutions, but its direct cause was the Napoleonic occupation of Spain. Some visionary patriots, the greatest of whom was Simón Bolívar, struggled intensely not only to liberate the colonies, but to create federations of countries. Nevertheless, and despite the political and military cooperation which was forthcoming during the wars against the colonial power, the Creole oligarchies of each former colony brought this cooperation to an end, and fomented local or border conflicts between the emerging states as a way of legitimising their claim to power.

The nations embarked upon their independent lives with extrovert policies, with the life of the economy being dominated heavily by the external sector, without changing the pre-existing socio-economic structures, and with weak states. These internal and external structures hampered the development of any spirit of enterprise, social change or technological innovation.

As a positive factor from the colonial period, in all Latin American countries, there had been a natural process of mixing with the indigenous peoples, and later with African peoples giving rise to cultural forms and artistic expressions of the highest value. In Latin America, the time/space relationship has always had, and continues to have a different dimension to the European one or the Anglo-American one. The way it is expressed in contemporary music, the plastic arts and literature is the witness to this cultural reality. Neruda, Garcia Marquez, Niemeyer, Guayasamin all respond in precise terms to this space/time concept defining the original personality of Latin America.

With the disappearance of Spain as a colonial power, Britain assumed a hegemonic role which, a century later, was to be taken on by the USA. Therefore, it is no exaggeration to say that in Latin America, there has been independence without decolonisation. Another consequence having profound effects has been the peripheral feeling which Latin American development has experienced. Apart from reasons of indigenous capital or climate, as in the cases of Quito, Bogota and Mexico City, capital and development are to be found, and take place on the coast or near the sea. In this aspect, the process in Latin America has been the opposite of that in the USA. In the latter country, the creative venture offered by its richness, and by its folklore, was the conquering of the West. On the other hand, in Latin America and particularly in South America, the conquest of the hinterland has not been a national aim of its peoples, except in Brazil, which, in an act of admirable political foresight, established the capital in the middle of the country, as an act of autonomy.

Cultural and political dependence

Considered together, the Latin American elites depended on Europe, and later on the USA in their concept of political life and planning.

Thus it is that as in the post-colonial period—the nineteenth century and a substantial part of the early twentieth century—democracy as established in all the constitutions, is superficial, weak and repeatedly repressed by military governments, except in Chile and Uruguay. Its progress has its roots in the agrarian oligarchies which copy models of European life, whilst commerce and what scant industry there is, is generally foreign-owned. Basically, economic life depends on mineral or vegetable raw materials which are exported.

Commercial pressure from Europe is constant, and even the blockading of ports has been used to obtain payment of debts, or to encourage internal conflicts in order to control the natural wealth or even to install emperors to satisfy European monarchies. Military intervention by the USA, particularly in the Caribbean and Central America, is frequent. In the economic field direct investment in mines, energy and transport is widespread, and since the First World War has preferentially been from the USA, which then came to share this role with Great Britain.

Successive crises and the present day

The crises of 1930 brought profound consequences, both socially and on the economic structure. The state starts directing the economy and creates basic industries. This process was accentuated during the Second World War owing to restrictions on imports, and industrial growth soared at that time.

In the 1940s, the first iron and steel plants were set up, energy and transport facilities were expanded, and through development plans, the state stimulated the birth of manufacturing industry and gave an impulse to social services. One of the great problems of Latin America over the last thirty years, has been to cope with the Industrial Revolution which Europe, the USA and Japan went through in the nineteeth century, and at the same time, the post-war technological revolution.

This effort modified the social structure very profoundly, created very strong educational requirements and financial demands which gave rise to chronic inflation processes. The democracy of the elite became a democracy of the middle class whilst popular demands grew.

In the 1950s, the first integration efforts were made, and continued until they were suspended by the military governments. In this situation, during the 1960s and 1970s, there was in many countries, a process of social crisis, of applying the doctrine of National Security driven on by the USA (which sees its only firm allies in the armies of Latin America), and later, under dictatorial regimes, the application of neo-liberal monetarist theories spreading outwards from the School of Economics at the University of Chicago.

The military experiments of Brazil, Uruguay, Argentina, Ecuador, Bolivia and Chile have been neo-colonial in character. Brazil has been an exception because during the last 20-year military dictatorship, it managed to consolidate its industrial strength and maintained the decision-making power of the state. In the other countries, military mismanagement has meant a considerable loss of autonomy, a negative distribution of national income, domination by transnational companies, and, as the political price, acute repression of human rights. These governments increased overseas dependency through massive indebtedness, and in general, have been the greatest historic failure in the region.

Therefore, the democratic renaissance of Argentina, Uruguay, Brazil, Bolivia and earlier, Peru and Ecuador, has meant the beginning of a new era for South America. All these governments were born in the midst of acute social and financial difficulties, but they are based on the democratic will of the people, and are led by high quality leaders. Only Chile remains bent to the will of a dictatorship, which is what has led it into greater external dependency, to economic crisis and to political repression.

The economic scenario

Main trends: change with uncertainty

On the economic level, the next decade appears dominated by a great uncertainty which may be characterised in the industrialised countries of the North by a loss of dynamism derived from the earlier process of growth which generated certain problems such as:

a) The existing imbalances in hegemonic political power, both internal and external, and the ways in which these imbalances are resolved, at least over the short term.

b) The presence of what has become known as a third Industrial Revolution, which is starting to emerge clearly, which is distinguished by strong technological innovation, and which has marked repercussions on the basic functioning of societies in changing the earlier pattern of production, consumption and international economic relations.

c) A strong growth of the inter-relationships between world economies (in goods, services and factors such as capital and labour) which makes it difficult to take 'national' decisions as they are likely not to solve the problems encountered, but rather to create others, even more serious if they do not maintain the necessary compatibility.

d) A very unequal share in access to sustained growth, in which the North has reached a hitherto unseen state of well-being, and in which very few countries of the South have managed to join. And in which, also, the main way of adjusting the economy is to impose even more uncertainty on the countries of the South. This is especially valid in the case of Latin America:

   i) Its high cumulative external debt which stands at around US$ 360,000 million in 1985, and which obliges this region to be an exporter of capital. That is to say, Latin America contributes towards solving the difficulties of the central economies;

   ii) High interest rates;

   iii) The sharp reduction in the inflow of private investment funds into the region;

   iv) The worsening of the terms of trade derived from loss of activity, such as the process of technological substitution; and,

   v) The new protectionism which militates against the growth of exports, and in particular, of those labour-intensive export products, with labour being the most plentiful resource, a phenomenon which assumes even greater proportions if you think about the direction of change in the USA, Japan and the EEC.

e) A series of crises in the field of international cooperation in which nearly all the multinational institutions created have shown a great inability to foresee and meet the requirements of the current situation.

Even this trend has been reinforced by decisions taken by the hegemonic powers and by the inability of other developed powers to accept a balanced international order.

The rest of the world does not assume the leadership, waiting, as it is for a simple recovery of the economy of the USA. Neither do the transnational companies appear as leaders capable of assuming this role. We stand by perplexed at the resurgence of bilateralism, when we are all convinced of the need for a different focus to bring about a change in international commercial, financial and monetary systems.

Latin America: paradox and rebirth

Latin America is a heterogeneous grouping of countries, some of which may be considered as vast economic units, others as medium-sized and many as rather small. In it, there are countries which have achieved a higher welfare level. The region is regarded as being of average level, but that, obviously, is a simplification which does not include all the cases.[1] Its efforts towards greater cooperation have always been present, although, it must be recognised, they may not always have been as effective as one might have wished. Various factors explain this fact, some international, some local, but without doubt, the most relevant factors have been:

a) *At local level*

   i) Our political differences based on a wide range of different and often opposing regimes: dictatorships versus democracies.

   ii) Our economic differences which derive from different economic focuses which favour opposing strategies which, in the majority of cases, tend to hinder regional cooperation and integration agreements.

   iii) A marked nationalism which seeks to set us up as nations on rather mistaken bases, such as the arms race and doctrines of national security; and the belief that we can obtain greater benefits from individual actions.

   These reasons have limited our capacity for joint action, and have led us to squander resources which could be very productive. Changing this outdated nationalistic concept is a central task if we are to achieve increasing regional cooperation and have additional resources available to sustain economic growth. The task of controlling the arms race should be given special priority, and is only possible within a national focus and one of cooperation with the main producing centres.

b) *At international level*

   i) Competition amongst the countries of the region for access to the benefits of international trade has weakened our negotiating capacity and favoured the rest of the world, particularly the negotiating capacity of those dominating countries which have been able to take advantage of our differences. It is at least curious that the most minute requirements of reciprocity are made, of a kind which are unheard of in negotiations between countries outside the region.

   ii) The belief, particularly during the last decade, in some ill-defined world growth, with an abundance of easily accessible financial resources, and a great capacity to penetrate overseas markets which leads us to believe, to a greater or lesser degree in this region, in miraculous and over-simplified solutions.

   iii) The existence of international systems and rules which are adverse for the countries of the region, and which were created especially to serve the relations and interests of the developed countries of the North. (IMF, GATT, the World Bank, etc.)

At the present time, we are aware, in spite of the failures of our regional cooperation, that, paradoxically, the international scenario obliges us to develop it as much as possible, in order to seek the room for manoeuvre which would allow us to meet the dramatic needs of our peoples; growth redistribution, higher employment, and a better quality of life.

The process of disinvestment which these countries have started to witness is tragic; thus, in the case of Chile, enquiries made recently show that one in every three university students plans to leave the country. Amongst the country's poor population, only one in every ten youths has enjoyed stable employment over the last ten years. The scarcity of external resources is dramatic: it has gone from an abundant superfluity to total scarcity. The loss of world-wide commercial dynamism and the cumulative foreign debt, have obliged us to sustain large deficits in our balance of payments making us into exporters of capital, leaving us without resources to invest and having to confine average consumption at unsatisfactory low levels.

Whilst the external creditors act in concert, we make only token joint actions which are promptly discredited by the developed countries within the international system. Further, those countries with a high percentage of private sector debt have been obliged to provide state guarantees for that debt. We are convinced that this problem should be faced in some other way. It is no longer just an economic problem but, clearly, a political one. This is due not only to mistakes on our part, but also to mistakes on the part of the emerging international banking system and on the part of a determined economic policy of hegemonic power. Nevertheless, the cost of these mistakes cannot be our responsibility alone; to accept that point of view would be to accept a new form of economic colonialism.

The external debt and possible policies.[2]

No other topic holds the attention of the region like that of the external debt. Only in recent weeks has President Alan Garcia of Peru announced that for a period of twelve months, his country would be paying only interest to a value not exceeding 10 per cent of exports, and the Lima Declaration refers to the 'unsustainable burden of servicing the external debt which is compromising the stability of democracy in the region'. As the declaration forming part of the Cartagena Consensus points out, meeting the demands of the current situation has 'called for substantial sacrifices of the standards of living of the Latin American peoples, which in some cases are approaching the outer limits', leading to a ratification of 'the determination of its governments not to allow a situation of enforced insolvency or continued economic stagnation to be precipitated'. 'Our countries will not accept these risks indefinitely,' adds the four-party declaration dated 9 May 1984, signed by President Raul Alfonsín, Joao Figueiredo, Belisario Betancur and Miguel de la Madrid. Similar concepts were voiced by President Sanguinetti in his letter to the Heads of State and Government of the seven main industrialised powers in Bonn, in May 1985. At the UN, the President of Brazil again made it clear that he would not pay the debt at the cost of poverty and underdevelopment in his country.

All that has been said in the last two years points to a broad political consensus in Latin America: the conditions of paying the foreign debt currently imposed on the region mean that it cannot continue much longer without serious risk to democratic continuity. This clamour of a whole continent goes systematically unheard by the industrialised world. Those benefiting from the current international order show a great short-sightedness.

It is in this context that the question is asked: What does dealing with the external debt in political terms mean? Everything seems to suggest that the first task is to significantly increase the region's negotiating powers. What is clear is that having justice on our part is not enough, it is also necessary to show political strength and collective decision in order to force negotiations which the industrialised world does not want.

The industrialised world cannot go on irresponsibly ignoring the fact that the economic terms imposed by the IMF are inevitably intended to weaken the fragile democracies which are the successors of the military regimes which blossomed throughout the region in the 1960s and 1970s, and to suffocate the more deeply-rooted amongst them. Faced with social polarisation and accentuated political tensions, the mechanisms of agreeing upon and identifying permanent national interests will become weakened. Behind all this, those with a nostalgic yearning for authoritarianism will raise their heads, and, as always, will see force as the best means of tackling the problem, hiding it behind repression and silence.

It is a fact that all the international agreements reached up till now with the International Monetary Fund have contributed towards increasing social polarisation and political tensions. It is this reality which turns the debt problem into an international political problem.

No country can legitimately be asked to put its own stability at risk to ensure the stability of the creditor banks. It is not politically possible. Democracy in Latin America has to be underwritten by social justice and solidarity. When this is what is at stake, to continue demanding the same conditions for the payment of the foreign debt is ethically illegitimate. To affirm this reality appears to be of the utmost importance.

What is being done with Latin America is not legitimate from an ethical and moral point of view, particularly if the following additional elements are considered:

- Drastic changes have been brought about in the international economic conditions under which the debt was contracted, without any of them being the responsibility of the debtor countries;
- The transnational banking system has not applied its own rules of the game concerning commercial risk; now it is insisting on state guarantees for private sector credit which was granted earlier without any public guarantee;
- A good part of the loans granted are now deposited in the creditor banks themselves. It is difficult to state the exact value of these funds which 'have already returned' to the industrialised world. The figures given vary from US $80–160 billion;
- The very lack of foresight of the creditor banks led to the crisis in which we find ourselves, as they did not accurately evaluate the repayment power of their public and private debtors; and,
- In a substantial number of countries, public credits were acquired by military governments which applied neo-liberal policies to stimulate international private sector indebtedness and removed protection from national industry.

All this does not seek to deny Latin America's responsibilities in the external debt crisis that she is going through, nor the will to adopt the internal measures which are needed to face up to national and international economic realities. Proof of this is to be found in the US$ 60,000 million worth of net capital exports which occurred in only two years, 1983 and 1984. But it should be understood that it is not possible, either politically or ethically to continue this way, and that a population of 350 million cannot be kept working to pay off the foreign debt, something which seen from Latin America is so obvious that it does not seem possible for the industrialised world not to see it in these terms. In the political sphere, all this resembles the financial payment conditions imposed on the defeated nations of the First World War by the Treaty of Versailles. They were so unreal, and so unworthy, that in the end, they created the conditions for another war.

Hence the need for insisting on the principle of joint responsibility. The foreign debt crisis is not the responsibility of the debtor countries alone. There is a joint responsibility involving in one form or another the International Monetary Fund, the World Bank, the governments of the creditor countries, the governments of the debtor countries, private and publicly-owned debtor companies, and very importantly, the large traditional transnational banks. Only if this joint responsibility were recognised would it be possible to find a realistic solution combining democratic stability with the stability of the international financial system. It should not be forgotten that nearly all the variables in the foreign accounts of Latin American countries depend on decisions being taken which are outside our control. Interest rates are fixed in the markets of the North and are strongly influenced by the fiscal deficits of the industrialised countries; equally, the price and volume of exports depend to a great extent on demand from these countries and their protectionist policies; the same occurs with the prices of imports; and, lastly, the volume of credits depends on the policy of the banks and the Monetary Fund.

Finally, going beyond whether or not the reasons given about the risks to democracy are accepted, the illegitimate nature of what is being done, and what evident joint responsibility there is, there remains one inescapable reality: the industrialised world is committing a great political error in its dealings with Latin America. Very few seem disposed to recognise this fact, except to say, one unsuspected voice: that of Henry Kissinger. In a recent article (*El Pais*, 10 July 1985), he described the current situation in the following terms, which owing to their importance, it may be helpful to quote *in extenso*:

The most important event at the recent 'summit' of the industrial democracies, held in Bonn, was not adequately analysed by the participants there, and neither did it receive the news coverage which it deserved. This was the letter signed by eleven heads of government of the main countries of Latin America, in which they were seeking the help of the participants, bearing in mind that the 'grave problems' of the Latin American crisis could not be solved solely by the nations suffering them.

The response of the industrialised countries was laden with protocol and evasive. They congratulated themselves, simply for the fact that the Latin American foreign debt problems 'although far from being solved' is being dealt with flexibly and in an effective way.

When the Presidents of the main Latin American countries make their voices heard jointly, and are ignored, political relations over the long term in the Western hemisphere are threatened.

What is the crisis to which these nations are referring? For the United States and the majority of the industrial democracies, the problem is none other than the excessive indebtedness of these Latin American countries, which, it is claimed, is being solved by the Western democracies, using traditional financial methods. But for the Southern neighbours of the United States, the question represents nothing less than the survival of their political institutions ... to ignore, or to trivialise the call made by eleven Latin American Presidents is, therefore, extremely dangerous.

The questions which are crucial—of life or death—for recent democratic governments, are handled by international bankers and officials who, however perspicacious they may be, never have sufficient authority or enough experience to know how to design relations of a political character.

Some conclusions

If the debt problem is solved with imagination and solidarity, Latin America would be in a position to begin a process of integration which would consolidate its democracy and its participation in the Western world. This process depends fundamentally on three factors:

1) That the extreme poverty which affects 20, 30 or 40 per cent of the population is eliminated, depending on the country, and that conditions of justice and participation for everybody be created. The democracy of the middle class has become a mass democracy.
2) That sustained economic growth be maintained.
3) That an intense programme of economic integration and political solidarity be launched, which would widen markets, reduce defence expenditure by solving border problems, and achieve concerted internal action.

If the process of democratisation is supported, Latin America, which is a rich, vast and rather empty continent, could experience extraordinary development. At the end of the century, with its 600 million inhabitants and its natural resources, it could be the most important partner of the USA and Europe. Its development calls for active cooperation today, eliminating the burden of the debt, and providing political respect and investment. Latin America wishes to remain outside the East–West conflict.

If there is no internal cooperation, and the USA and Europe continue their restrictive, hegemonic policies, the failure of the democratic forces of Latin America could create in the region a serious threat to world peace, and a direct threat to the security of the Western world. Cooperation with this process nevertheless requires that the sovereignty and development style of each individual country be respected so that they respond to their real needs and individual cultures.

Notes

1. Latin America showed great expansion of production between 1950 and 1980, with figures showing the great dynamism of these countries' economies (5.7 per cent), which, taking account of population growth (2.7 per cent) leaves a substantial net figure when compared with historical patterns.
2. Many of the concepts about the debt are taken from the document prepared by the ILET for the seminar on Political Cooperation held in Montevideo on 16 August 1985.

Asia: the experience of the sub-continent

Altaf Gauhar

I

The process of decolonisation in the Indian sub-continent is a microcosm of the Asian experience. India witnessed the growth of nationalism; its division into two nationalist streams in the mid-1930s resulting in the partitioning of the sub-continent into two independent sovereign national states (India and Pakistan) in 1947; the emergence of Bengali nationalism and the conversion, through a popular armed resistance movement, of the eastern wing of East Pakistan into a third sovereign state of Bangladesh in 1972. It also witnessed the growth of the middle class and the active participation of the masses in the struggle for independence under the banner of nationalism, although the eventual transfer of power was to an elitist class which has maintained its domination in all three countries. India has been able to retain a formal democratic structure but Pakistan and Bangladesh have succumbed to military rule. For the masses, independence brought little change and they still remain an object of exploitation chained to the same British-style institutions which the ruling elites manipulate and control to consolidate their privileged position and to advance their interests. If an equitable and just social order is not created at the national level through popular participation, the people will strive to establish such orders at the regional and sub-regional level, leading to further fragmentation in all three countries.

India was the first colony to attain independence through a process of negotiations between the political leaders of India and the Imperial Government. There were political demonstrations, organised protests, frequent riots, acts of terrorism, and a great deal of bloodshed before independence was achieved, but the forces of nationalism in India never organised themselves into an armed resistance movement against colonial rule at any time. The triumph of nationalism in India was primarily the result of the gradual erosion and weaking of the colonial structures in India which virtually collapsed towards the end of the Second World War. In the end, it was the unacceptable cost of governing India that persuaded the British to cut their losses and quit. Admittedly, the middle class had been politicised during the inter-war years and a number of eminent individuals, educated in England, had returned home imbued with nationalist ideas and democratic ideals to lead the people in their struggle for independence. Many of the leaders were lawyers by training, which made them natural negotiators whose habitat was the court or the conference room rather than guerrilla camps and underground training centres. The bureaucratic institutions established by the British were run almost entirely by a class of Indian who were, as Lord Macaulay had hoped in 1835, 'Indian in blood and colour but English in taste, opinions, morals and intellect.' All this created the setting and the mechanism for the attainment of independence through negotiations rather than confrontation.

The British-style institutions and the structure of the ruling class has largely remained unchanged since independence. Political leaders still come from the same professions and families who acquired wealth and eminence during the colonial period. Since power was transferred to the old ruling class, it had a vested interest in perpetuating the British institutions. For the masses, the achievement of independence was the end of their struggle and also the end of their dreams. They passionately believed that once independence was achieved life would change for the better; in this belief they suffered and sacrificed beyond the limits of endurance. During the struggle the leaders had exhorted the people to sink their differences or, at least, put them aside until the goal of independence was reached. Any dissension or division in the ranks, they claimed, would weaken the struggle and postpone the arrival of independence.

The same approach was adopted by leaders of freedom movements elsewhere. Kwame Nkrumah of Ghana said 'Seek you first the political kingdom and all things will be added to you.' Julius Nyerere of Tanzania said in 1978 that African leaders genuinely believed that the attainment of independence would solve all problems, hence they did not work out any programmes for social and economic development in the post-colonial period, for such programmes would have caused differences and divisions. Independence was the primary condition, everything else was secondary. It was a puffy magic carpet which bore leaders in India to their political kingdoms.

Nationalism began as a great unifying force in India and ended as a highly divisive ideology. What was offered as an all-embracing dream of Indian nationhood dissolved at its first contact with the reality of power. The moment it became possible to obtain offices and positions of authority through the political process, class loyalties, group associations, religious differences all began to assert themselves. The most dramatic event occurred in 1937 when the All India National Congress formed governments in those provinces where the Muslims were in a majority. Government meant patronage and the Muslims soon discovered that patronage under a Hindu-dominated regime followed a parochial and communal route which by-passed them. Even in regions where the Muslims were in a majority they could not expect a fair deal from the Congress government. After 1937 two distinct streams of national-ism developed, one dominated by the Hindus, still claiming the ideology of a united secular Indian nation, and the other asserting its separate national status and seeking security in a state of its own composed of provinces where the Muslims were in a majority.

II

Pakistan was established as a sovereign state on the rising wave of Muslim nationalism. What could be more natural than for members of the same faith to form a nation-state of their own, where internal problems and differences would easily be resolved? The reality proved to be much harsher than the comfort of the illusion. Pakistan was composed of five provinces, four in the western part of India and one in the eastern part, separated by a distance of 1200 miles. Of the total population, 56 per cent lived in the province of East Pakistan. The new nation had a small bureaucratic class, a negligible armed force and no industrial base. The majority province of East Pakistan was entirely agrarian, with nothing in the way of business or industry except petty traders and shopkeepers.

During their struggle for independence—led by the All-India Muslim League—the Muslims emphasised every point of cultural, religious and economic difference with the majority Hindu community, and suppressed every division and distinction among the Muslims themselves. What the Indian National Congress discovered in 1937 when Congress governments assumed power, the Muslim League was to discover ten years later when the government of Pakistan came into existence. Nationalism was a potent force to guide the struggle for independence but once that goal was reached nationalism could serve neither as a cover to conceal social and economic disparities and inequities nor embank the tides of regional autonomous pressures.

In his first address to the Pakistan Constituent Assembly, the founder of Pakistan, Quaid-i-Azam, Mahomed Ali Jinnah, said that the whole world was wondering at the 'unprecedented cyclonic revolution' which had brought about the establishment of two independent sovereign nations in the sub-continent: 'There is no parallel in the history of the world.' Independence had been achieved peacefully and through 'an evolution of the greatest possible character.' He recognised that there were people who did not quite agree with the division of India but in his judgement there was 'no other solution'. He added, 'Maybe that view is correct; maybe it is not; that remains to be seen.' He called upon the people of Pakistan to 'work together in a spirit that everyone of you, no matter to what community he belongs, no matter what relations he has had with you in the past, no matter what is his colour or creed, is first, second and last a citizen of this state with equal rights, privileges and obligations ...'[1]

His hope was that the struggle for the establishment of Pakistan based on the separate cultural identity of the Muslims having reached its culmination, citizens of the new state would learn to forget the past and proceed to live together, Hindus and Muslims alike, as equal citizens. It was his judgement that the 'angularities' between Hindus and Muslims would vanish as would the regional distinctions between Pushtoons, Punjabis, Sindhis, Baluchis, and Bengalis: 'In course of time Hindus would cease to be Hindus and Muslims would cease to be Muslims, not in the religious sense, because that is the personal faith of each individual, but in the political sense as citizens of the state.'

He did not live long enough to see the resurgence of regional, parochial, and class conflicts and the sharpening and accentuation of 'the diacritical, differential, and monopolisable traits of the privileged groups';[2] the betrayal of his message that the nation 'should wholly and solely concentrate on the well-being of the people, and especially of the masses and the poor'. When an equitable national order failed to evolve with the full participation and support of the people, regional and class loyalties and identities resurfaced and submerged the national identity which had failed to secure popular adherence on the basis of mutual rights and obligations.

III

The question has been asked how a political struggle conducted under the banner of Muslim nationalism failed to create a national consciousness and culture. One reason is that nationalism meant all things to all people, and while political leaders employed the language of nationalism they never seriously studied the origins of nationalism and the structure of nation-states. Nationalism meant freedom and a promise of change. But that is the object not the content of nationalism.

The complex process through which individuals and groups came to subdue and partially surrender group loyalties and assume a national identity never claimed the attention of the politician. Even today it is not recognised that a national consciousness cannot be created by decree. The survival of a nation-state is assured not by the state enforcing patriotism and unity through arbitrary legislation but by the citizens recognising the benefit of belonging to the state as distinct from any smaller regional entity. A nation comes into existence when its citizens recognise mutual rights and duties to each other in virtue of their shared membership of it. As Ernest Gellner says, 'Having a nation is not an inherent attribute of humanity.' Nor is nationalism a state of human existence. A nation-state represents a political framework to which members of a community belong on equal terms in recognition of mutual rights and duties and in the expectation of mutual gain. Nationhood is acquired not ordained. A Bangladesh national who took part in the struggle for Pakistan in the 1940s has changed his identity three times. He started as an Indian citizen and became a Pakistani citizen in 1947, and then successfully struggled to acquire his Bangladesh citizenship in 1972. If citizenship which is an essential attribute of nationality was a human condition he should have been deprived of some quality with the loss of his two earlier identities. But he emerged a stronger and more liberated citizen each time. What drove the Muslims of India to seek a homeland of their own was the conviction that they would not obtain justice in a united India and that they would remain subject to Hindu domination and exploitation. It was the same sense of injustice and insecurity and the fear of continued repression and exploitation which drove the Bengali Muslims to separate from Pakistan and to establish a nation-state of their own. The Bengalis came to regard Pakistan nationalism as an instrument of domination and an alibi for injustice and oppression. They revolted against it and sought refuge in Bengali nationalism.

Three broad conclusions emerge from this:

1) The struggle for freedom in the sub-continent was conducted under the spirit of nationalism but this spirit did not survive once independent nation-states came into existence. Since independence did not provide security or equality, which was what the struggle was all about, nationalism came to be seen as a device to perpetuate existing inequitable social and economic structures.

2) Nation-states were created before a national consciousness representing a genuine fusion of polity and culture and an environment of homogeneity had come into existence. It was left to the state to create national consciousness. But the state structure was itself dominated by class interests and became the custodian of an inequitable social order.

3) When cultural homogeneity and a truly national consciousness failed to evolve, people began to revert to the security of their traditional class identities.

IV

Colonialism did not sponsor nationalism, though the process of decolonisation resulted in the emergence of nation-states. In that sense there is an interrelationship between colonialism, decolonisation and nationalism. Nation-states were not discovered by pioneers of nationalism, they were invented in response to a novel complex of social, economic and political needs and circumstances. These circumstances arose out of the European Industrial Revolution when agrarian social structures became an obstacle to growth and, through a gradual and often painful process, smaller self-sufficient communities developed into larger inter-dependent cultural units. Self-sufficiency at the village level was replaced by interdependence at the factory level as a result of growing specialisation. The transition occurred not because nationalism was embraced as a new religion or philosophy—indeed, there is little philosophy in the literature on nationalism—but because new economic demands and conditions forced the people to abandon parochial isolation and seek broader associations. And nation-states came to represent the optimum viable and collectively beneficial unit of cultural association.

When India emerged as the largest democracy in the world and Pakistan as the largest Muslim nation they were still in the agrarian stage of development. The social order was determined by caste and class, and the individual's need for security and well-being, however unjust the arrangement, were still best assured by a vast network of religious, sectarian and professional associations. The compulsions of interdependence had not yet challenged the effectiveness of these parochial structures. During the colonial period the Imperial Government had taken every step to heighten and exploit linguistic, sectarian and religious distinctions. The British wanted India's unity for administrative purposes but not an Indian unity which could have posed a threat to the Raj. The original census reports divided the population into Hindu and non-Hindu, agrarian and non-agrarian, male and female. By the end of the nineteenth century, every single sect was specifically accounted for, every linguistic and dialectical variation recorded, and details of every caste, its location and occupation meticulously described.

The first task of political leadership in independent India and Pakistan was to mobilise the masses in a fundamental restructuring of the social and economic order, in order to rid it of colonial modes of exploitation and to make it just and equitable, thus opening the possibilities of the growth of homogeneous cultural affiliations at the national level. This task they singularly and uniformly failed to address, let alone discharge. Why? Because the leadership itself was a product of the colonial period and acted more as middle-men than reformers or revolutionaries determined to bring about any radical change in the social order. They were the legatees of the British power and that meant the British institutions which they set out to preserve in order to consolidate their inheritance. These institutions had little meaning for the masses, but for the ruling classes they were the essence of power and the means to sustain and perpetrate their power. The judges wanted their wigs and robes, the lawyers their silk and Halsbury's *Laws of England*, and the teachers the English language as the medium of instruction. Army officers cherished British ranks and colours. The air force in Pakistan called itself the 'Royal Pakistan Air Force', and the 'Royal Pakistan Navy' followed suit.

A popular slogan during the struggle for independence was *Inqilab* meaning revolutionary change. But it did not take long for the people to discover that all they had changed was the colour of their masters; instead of white they now had brown rulers. Their fortunes did not change, nor did their conditions of work, for they remained doomed to submit to the domination of the same class which had been the principal instrument of the Raj. Those who had occupied positions of intermediate control under the British now assumed primary control. Any demand for change was treated as subversion and punished as such. A whole range of repressive statutes introduced by the British to control the expression of ideas, political activity and the press were retained, and in some cases made more stringent. The state employed every means at its disposal to obstruct and impede the evolution of a national consciousness in order to preserve its dominant class interests. The army in Pakistan ousted the effete political ruling group and assumed control of the state apparatus and the monopoly of state patronage and privileges ten years after independence. Over the years it has strengthened its hold and expanded its area of control to cover all fields of social and economic activities. It provides the country not only with soldiers and statesmen but also with short-story writers, humourists, and more recently, poets of considerable local renown. The same is true of Bangladesh, (General Irshad, the President of Bangladesh, is a poet of no ordinary merit) despite the fact that the nation was established through a prolonged political struggle that in its final phase became an armed struggle. In India, the democratic structures survive largely because the leadership has had the courage to go to the people periodically to renew its mandate but the social order is plagued with corruption and injustice, which threatens the growth of a genuinely democratic environment. The alienation of the Sikhs in the Punjab and their demand for an autonomous Sikh state is a serious threat to India's unity. The Gurkhas in Darjeeling too are agitating for greater autonomy though they have been temporarily 'clobbered' into silence.

V

What of the future? Many of the problems faced by the post-colonial state in the sub-continent of India confront other newly independent countries in the Third World with equal if not greater force. A class of Western politicians and academics is beginning to suggest that colonial rule was not such a bad thing after all. Lord Caradon claimed a few years ago that the free parliaments, independent courts and uncorrupted civil services left behind by the British in their former colonies had been destroyed by the politicians after independence. What free parliament did the British leave behind, and where? And which courts? The ones in India conducted their proceedings under laws made by the British and in a language which, in many cases, neither the plaintiff nor the defendant adequately understood, and the civil services were dominated by persons thoroughly alienated from their own culture. One must remember the motivations of the colonial power in distorting and subverting the process of decolonisation before one begins to see failure of national institutions in the post-colonial period as evidence of some congenital incapacity among the people of the Third World to administer their affairs in a participatory democratic manner. The evils of colonialism did not die with the unfurling of a multi-colour flag of independence often designed by the outgoing governor. (Lord Mountbatten spent days designing the national flag of Pakistan and was most upset when it was not accepted because he had planted the British Crown right in the centre, or so the story goes.)

The independent post-colonial state was conceived and created as a dependency, attached to the periphery of an economic system which guaranteed its systematic exploitation, and it was designed to remain subordinate to the metropolitical will. It sprang out of a vast marsh of violence, intrigue, and manipulation, and remains bogged down by external threats and domestic squabbles and contradictions. The seeds of disintegration were all sown in the colonial period. They are now coming to bitter fruition.

VI

The Third World is not alone in facing a threat of the dissolution of the nation-state. This is a threat which small and medium-sized powers and nations now face equally. They may not realise or they may not wish to recognise it but their sovereignty is being nibbled away; no, being gobbled away by chunks. State after state has been reduced to the position of a client state, a lackey, or at least an ally.

Now this represents the weakening not only of the system but the weakening of the whole structure of the nation-state and the international consensus which has kept the nation-states alive. At one end there was this whole process of fragmentation and the appearance of not only just many states or micro-states, but even states which one should call 'terminal states', states whose destiny and whose tourist economies are dependent not on the goodwill of the World Bank or the IMF, but on the goodwill of one travel agent in New York. This is enough to describe the economy of these countries. Together with the process of fragmentation was the monstrous acquisition of enormous power by a few states.

Not so long ago the world saw nationalism convert itself into a monstrous force of expansionism, racism, and fascism. One by one, nation-states were wiped off the map by fascist hordes in Europe, Asia and Africa. It was the combined will and might of all the democratic and socialist nations which vanquished fascism. The victorious nations enshrined in the UN Charter their resolve to respect and uphold the territorial integrity of all nations, large or small. The Charter guaranteed the sovereignty of states and outlawed aggression and interference in the internal affairs of states. It also provided that people should have the right to self-determination so that they may be assured of freedom and human rights. This was the environment of international obligations in which the process of decolonisation began. Had the imperial powers honourably discharged their obligations under the Charter and relinquished their colonial hold, the world would have seen the emergence of genuinely independent and viable nation-states. The Third World would not have been carved up in such an arbitrary and merciless manner. But decolonisation was not the result of any change of heart nor was it undertaken in fulfilment of the obligations assumed by the imperial powers under the Charter. Decolonisation had become an economic necessity. And the imperial powers withdrew from their colonies only after they had ensured that their strategic and commercial interests would be preserved and advanced. If that were not so, at least some nation-states after decolonisation would have succeeded in improving the living conditions of the masses in a fundamental and constructive sense. The often cited examples of Taiwan, Hong Kong, South Korea and Singapore are ludicrous. Two of them are not even nation-states; a third is under effective US control; and the fourth is but a show-window of the multinationals.

We talk of an interdependent world and hope that the dictates of inter-dependence might help us advance from nationalism to internationalism. The reality is that with every passing day we are going back on our obligations as nation-states under the Charter. When a government invades the territory of another sovereign state in retaliation for a crime allegedly commited to a third country and the act is seen by a superpower as legitimate self-defence, what must one make of the notion of the sovereignty of nation-states? When millions of people are expelled from their homeland and massacred wherever they happen to find refuge the right of self-determination becomes a mockery. When a small minority subjugates through indescribable brutalities millions of people in their own country and consigns them to sub-human existence because of the colour of their skin it makes mankind ashamed of itself. And what of a small country in Central America under constant waves of supersonic threats every hour of the day? The concept of national sovereignty was never so recklessly flouted as in recent weeks when a nuclear nation with a proud civilization (France) cynically planned an act of state terrorism to destroy a 'Greenpeace' vessel on a mission of peace. National sovereignty, national integrity, the right not to interfere in the internal affairs of other states, nation-states—big, medium and small—have all been reduced to 'paper states'. Their sovereignty is now deeply curtailed, their freedom of action severerely circumscribed.

In answer to a question from a journalist in Paris in October 1985, Mr Mikhail Gorbachov replied 'You can put such questions to other nations, not to the Soviet Union.' Now we are all 'other nations' which means nations that can be insulted and bullied. The superpowers have the means to destroy us all. They maintain what they call 'the balance of terror'. The balance is in their favour, the terror is all ours. The rights of other nations are of no concern to them. It is their national interest, their strategic purpose, their tactical design and their propaganda ploys that matter. The rest of the world has earned for itself the role of helpless spectators. Grenada can be invaded and occupied as easily as Afghanistan. Fascism never presented the kind of threat that the might and mood of the superpowers presents to the world today. For us both have established their own 'empire of evil' which will remain evil so long as they retain any nuclear arms. The nuclear powers, the superpowers, have imposed on the globe a regime which can only be described as 'nuclear apartheid'. The superpowers belong to a world apart, and they hold every other nation in thrall. Unity and collective action by all nations of the world, particularly like-minded nations, has now become an imperative of survival. If they continue to submit to 'nuclear apartheid' they will be denied every human value, every human right that they cherish, and mankind will be exposed to wanton destruction.

Notes

1. *Speeches as Governor-General of Pakistan: Jinnah 1947–48*, Karachi: Pakistan Publications, 1949.
2. Ernest Gellner, *Nations and Nationalists*, Oxford: Basil Blackwell, 1983, p11.

China: the lessons of development

He Liliang

Mr Chairman, distinguished representatives, ladies and gentlemen

First of all, I would like to express my thanks to the Vienna Institute for Development and *South* magazine for kindly inviting me to this symposium on 'Decolonisation and After'.

This month marks the fortieth anniversary of the UN and the twenty-fifth anniversary of the Declaration on the granting of independence to colonial countries and peoples. This makes our gathering here all the more significant. The UN itself signifies the triumph of the world's peace-loving forces over fascism. In the past forty years, tremendous changes have taken place on the international scene, and colonialism as a system has been rendered a thing of the past by the upsurge of national independence movements. As a result of the emergence of more than one hundred newly-independent countries and active participation of a large number of small and medium-size countries in the world political arena, the pattern of international relations has been drastically transformed, the forces against war strengthened, and the process of decolonisation integrated with the world movement for democracy and progress. At present, the peoples of the world are making continued efforts to enhance the role of the UN and to bring about a better world.

However, while we have reason to rejoice over forty years of peace in the post-war period and the achievements of decolonisation, there is still cause for grave concern. Hot spots fomented by big and small expansionists continue to plague the world. Foreign aggression against the military occupation of Namibia, Palestine and other Arab territories, as well as Afghanistan and Kampuchea constitute a gross violation of the purposes and principles of the UN Charter as well as an open defiance to the cause of decolonisation. Such acts of power politics have been strongly condemned by the UN General Assembly and international public opinion. We hold that no country should be allowed to violate the sovereignty of its neighbours or to impose military occupation on the territories of others. The withdrawal of occupation troops is the essential prerequisite for any political settlement. As long as aggression and foreign occupation are not eliminated from the earth, we cannot close the file of decolonisation.

Mr Chairman, imperialist and colonialist oppression and exploitation brought untold suffering to China in the past. The triumph of the Chinese people's revolution in 1949 was the outcome of a protracted struggle against imperialism and colonialism. Only after the founding of New China, did the Chinese people achieve genuine national independence and become masters of the land.

A common question facing the developing countries after their political independence, is whether or not they can consolidate their independence through economic development. This is also the case with China, a member of the South.

In order to rid the country of extreme poverty and illiteracy, the Chinese people have made tremendous efforts since 1949 for social and economic development. Our people have demonstrated an enormous enthusiasm and spirit of dedication, and have practised frugality; a national economy based on socialist public ownership was instituted in the first thirty years after the liberation. We have established a fairly comprehensive industrial system and other sectors necessary for economic and social development. Noticeable progress in the fields of industry, agriculture, scientific research, education and public health was achieved. Some four hundred thousand state and collective enterprises have been set up in the sectors of industry, agriculture and communications, etc. Among them over 8,000 are of large and medium scale, which provide more than 95 per cent of the capital goods, energy and consumer goods that the country needs. China's per capita national income was tripled. The rate of adult illiteracy and semi-literacy in the total population has been reduced from 60 per cent in the early 1950s to 20 per cent at the end of the 1970s. The build-up of China's economic strength is beyond doubt in the interest of peace and progress of the world.

It should be noted, nevertheless, that our economic and social development has not run a straight course and we have acquired both positive and negative experiences.

Faced with the situation of underdevelopment of the motherland, every Chinese patriot would naturally be anxious to lift the country from the state of 'poverty and blankness'. Unfortunately, the 'left' errors hindered our economy for a considerable period of time after 1958, especially during the so-called 'Cultural Revolution' from 1966 to 1976. The left errors had led the country into a bad situation, because they were not in keeping with the objective conditions of the country and have surpassed the present level of economic and social development and the level of people's political consciousness. We have learned a profound lesson.

Summing up the past experience, we have realised that we must integrate our theories of socialism with the concrete realities of China; we must take our own road and build a socialism with Chinese characteristics. This idea is the guiding principle for modernising China. In carrying out our modernisation programme we must proceed from Chinese realities.

In 1978, the Party and the government made the decision to shift the focus of the nation's work to economic and social development and to lay the indispensable material foundation for building China into a prosperous modern socialist country with a high level of democracy and civilisation. A great goal was set for the modernisation of our national economy, namely, to quadruple China's GNP in 20 years by the end of the century. Taking into account the deep-rooted problems in our economic management system, the state has resolved, while upholding socialism and the principle of central planning, to launch major reforms in the country's economic system, to revitalise the national economy, and to pursue an 'open door' policy, so as eventually to establish a socialist economic system with Chinese characteristics.

The main points of our current reform are to relax the rigid supervision by the state over the enterprises; to give more emphasis to the law of value and the role of the market; and to eliminate absolute egalitarianism in the distribution system. The reforms started in the rural area where 80 per cent of the population reside. We have changed the structure of the rural economy which was incompatible with the development of the forces of production in agriculture and have introduced the system of contracted responsibility for production with remuneration linked to output, thus bringing into play the enormous enthusiasm of our peasants for developing agriculture. Since then, individuals, households or small collectives have formed their own accounting units for distributing their income, so that the peasants' income is directly linked with their performances of work; no more is there the practice of everybody eating from the big pot of the commune. The peasants can make their own choice as to what to plant according to the state planning guidance, instead of previous mandatory instructions, and they are allowed to sell their products in the market, which was formerly forbidden. As a natural outcome of the responsibility system and other reforms, the agricultural products all of a sudden have become plentiful, and the income of the rural population has increased rapidly. All this has led to a greater interflow between industry and agriculture and between urban and rural areas, thus facilitating the development of the overall national economy.

The success of rural reforms has provided a solid material basis for national economic and social development and laid the foundation for further reforms of the overall economic structure of the country.

Last year, the state decided to continue the reforms, aiming at an all-round restructuring of the main aspects of the economic system such as planning, credit, taxation, wage and the price system. Special emphasis is made to revitalise urban enterprises, to increase their economic returns, to develop commodity production and to bring about a rise in the revenues of the government, so as to ensure greater achievements in the modernisation of our national economy. I would like to elaborate upon just a few aspects of this:

The main tasks for the rural economic reforms include the following:

1) To make the urban enterprises, which account for one million units and play a very important role in our economy, truly independent economic entities, and to eliminate the widespread bad practice of distribution of income, in order to bring into fuller play the vitality of rural enterprises and initiative of the workers. This implies a proper sharing of responsibilities, rights, interests and benefits between the state, the enterprises and workers and to improve their efficiency, so that the state will no longer be the 'big pot' for the enterprises, which in turn will no longer serve as the 'big pot' for the workers. The crucial point here is that the state should loosen its direct supervision over the enterprises, resort to economic and legal means, and take administrative measures only when it is absolutely necessary. To ensure smooth progress of the reforms, the government should improve its own management methodology in planning and fully utilise fiscal, taxation, pricing, wage, banking, auditing, statistical and other macro-economic instruments, in order to exercise control and coordination of the national economy.

2) The enterprises should be given greater decision-making power in such areas as production planning, marketing, pricing, procurement of materials, use of financial resources, personnel matters, wages and bonus issues, etc, which the enterprises did not possess in the past. As to the workers, their income is determined by their work performance and is closely related to the operation of the enterprises. Only by adopting all the above-mentioned measures can we get rid of the persistent absolute egalitarianism in our distribution system and introduce incentives into our enterprises.

3) To carry out reform in the pricing system, which is the key issue of the reform.

For a long period, the prices of products were fixed by the government. With the passing of time and the interaction of the various factors of economic development, this system of freezing of prices eventually separated prices from the value of the products and neglected the factor of supply and demand. Consequently, the prices did not reflect the true performance in production and an accurate calculation of costs and productivity was impossible. Besides, the prices of manufactured goods were much higher than those of raw materials, and heavy industrial products earned much more profits than light industrial products. For this reason, some products were kept too long in stock as their quality, type and price did not meet the requirements of the society, while others were out of supply. Therefore, our reform of the pricing system will lay greater emphasis on the role of the market mechanisms in making the economy more dynamic and the price lever should be used to eliminate the above-mentioned irrationalities, which have hindered economic development.

Parallel to the measures of pricing reforms is the government decision to carry out a reform of the wage system, to encourage better work and higher initiatives and creativeness of the workers and the intellectuals. With the implementation of these measures of reform, production will expand steadily and the people's living standards will be further improved.

4) To carry out the 'open door' policy. This policy pursued in the last few years is also an important part of our efforts to correct the 'leftism' and to reform the economic structure. It is the lesson of the past one hundred years or so that the policy of closing the country to international intercourse only results in a state of backwardness. We will hardly be able to achieve the goals of modernisation by the end of this century without making use of the financial resources and the advanced technology of other countries.

In formulating our policy towards foreign financial resources, we used to believe that it is comforting to have no foreign debts. However, we did not realise that the proper use of foreign capital has an important supplementary role to play in developing the country's productivity and improving the management of our enterprises. It is beyond doubt that self-reliance remains the guiding principle of our economic construction; it is equally clear that our 'open door' policy will be long-lasting and unswerving.

In order to pursue the 'open door' policy, to make fuller use of foreign capital and to import technology, a crucial issue is to increase our foreign exchange earnings through the export expansion. Efforts are being made to reorient our exports from raw materials and primary products to manufactured goods. At the same time, invisible trade will be vigorously promoted. With a view to facilitating the implementation of the 'open door' policy, China has designated some special economic zones and coastal open cities, providing a measure of favourable treatment to foreign investment. Legislative work is also under way to formulate laws and regulations governing joint ventures and other forms of economic cooperation. Our principle in this regard is equality and mutual benefit.

Since 1979, the economic reforms in China have already brought about encouraging results. China is now self-sufficient in food and has a surplus of cotton. Varieties of light industrial products have increased. The market is brisk. There is an upturn in government revenues. Some thirty million people in the urban areas have obtained jobs. Staff and workers' average actual income has increased by 20 per cent, and the average income of the 800 million rural population by 80 per cent. National income is growing at an annual rate of 7 per cent.

Though we have achieved good results, we are well aware that China is still backward in its economy and the per capita GNP is only around US $300, so our people are determined to work harder to reach the goal of modernisation.

Mr Chairman, in conducting our 'open door' policy and expansion of international economic relations, we are encountering various external obstacles.

First, international trade conditions are not favourable.

It is quite difficult for China's commodities, especially semi-manufactured goods and industrial products, to enter into some major countries of the North, because of the high tariffs imposed on our commodities and other protectionist measures against our exports. As a result, our foreign trade earning is still very small in terms of a per capita figure, and we have a long-standing unfavourable balance of trade with them. Like other developing countries, China suffers from the down-turn of commodity prices and protectionist measures. We wish to call upon these Northern countries to pursue more far-sighted policies so as to roll back trade protectionism, establish a just and equitable international economic order, enhance cooperation between the North and the South, and thus to assist the growth of the world economy. Secondly, the transfer of technology also comes across numerous difficulties.

At present, when China is preparing the ground for an economic take-off in the next decade, technological transformation for thousands of factories is required. Regrettably, many transnational corporations and the governments concerned are only interested in selling manufactured goods to us; they are not willing to transfer their technology and know-how to us and they demand an excessively high price for the transfer of patent. Quite often, licences for some technologies have to pass prolonged examination in COCOM. It is our hope and that of many other developing countries, I am sure, that the industrialised countries will offer reasonable and favourable terms regarding the transfer of technology. We believe that the development of the economy of China and other developing countries will certainly have a marked favourable effect on the economy of the industrialised countries in the North.

Thirdly, as interest rates on the international money market and of the World Bank remain rather high, far above the rate of earnings of hard currency of China's enterprises in general, we have to refrain from seeking large loans from abroad even when we are short of financial resources. We hope that the North will provide more official development assistance and more concessional loans to the developing countries, and in the first place to the least developed countries.

Mr Chairman, before concluding my remarks, I would like to mention a possible question: whether China's reforms will lead to the restoration of capitalism. The fact is that over 90 per cent of the enterprises in China are state owned; no transaction of land and other important means of production is allowed, the Party and the Government stress socialist ethics while promoting material civilisation, and our people support and uphold the socialist system. The commodity economy in our socialist society is developed under the guidance of the central planning. Even if the individual economy and the involvement of foreign capital is on the increase, the nature of China's social-economic formation will remain socialist and the bourgeoisie as a class will never re-emerge in China.

In short, the present reform in China is a great experiment in the most populous developing country of the world, aimed at casting off underdevelopment. We believe that the reform is in the right direction and is supported by the people. Though we still face a lot of difficulties, we are fully confident in the bright future of reform. I know that the question of China's reform and development strategy is attracting much interest of the international community and I shall be glad to share my views about it with the distinguished representatives present here.

Finally, allow me to express once again my heartfelt thanks to our hosts and *South* magazine for their hospitality.

Thank you.

The future is upon us

Bruno Kreisky

Mr Chairman

I am afraid that what I am going to say will fall short of the profundity that marked the statements of our eminent friends and I must say again that I am most grateful to you for having undertaken this long journey to Vienna to participate in this conference. I should like to thank our friends from *South* magazine who decided to cooperate with us because this has added stature to this conference. I should also like to thank all those who spoke yesterday. Even for one who for more than twenty-five years, almost thirty years, has dealt with these matters, a good many of the things that were said yesterday have meant a most valuable enrichment of my knowledge. I for one learned a lot yesterday.

What I am going to say will be different from what was said yesterday, as I have already said, by a certain lack of profoundness, and I shall try to be as frank as possible. A great French catholic author once said '*Je suis ici pour dire la verité, et un homme dit la verité quand il dit ce qu'il pense.*' ('I am here to speak the truth, and one speaks the truth when one says what one thinks.') And it is in this spirit that I should like to give you my subjective truth as I see it.

From the very beginning I considered 'the new economic order' a very unfortunate formula, a formula which all of a sudden entered the political limelight thanks to the UN. I think that it is a formula which was badly chosen. But, understandably, Third World countries, which do not share our experiences as far as political seminars are concerned, adopted it.

I have been a social democrat for more than fifty years and I have learned, particularly during the years after the Second World War, that there is nothing that irritates the conservative and the liberals more than if we social democrats speak of a new economic order within our own domestic economies. In such times as we live in, the policy of instituting a new economic order is not one for which one can gain popular support. Such formulas, on the contrary, tend to have an adverse effect and from the very beginning I considered it to be unfortunate that the conservative and liberal forces in the world, important as they are, particularly in the field of business, should be confronted with a term which is an abomination to them in domestic politics where things are much less problematic. Quite typical of the thinking of the conservatives and the liberals in terms of development aid, in fact very typical, was the intervention of the Swiss delegate at the 1984 UNIDO conference here in Vienna. The Swiss delegate had quite clearly proposed on behalf of all important liberal and conservative forces (partly even social democrats perhaps) in very concrete terms, an order such as he foresaw with regard to developing countries. It was a statement which was such a far cry from reality that I was greatly taken aback. What he said—and this was applauded by most of the other European representatives—was basically an outflow of Manchester Liberalism in respect to the Third World, with hardly any adaptation to reality.

We have seen that the expression 'new economic order' has not met with any response in the world, and endeavours to discuss this in fora other than very limited circles has again and again found this. The last time was in Cancún. Although I was one of the co-chairmen there my health prevented me from participating in that meeting, but whatever I have heard about Cancún has convinced me that it was a very kind and friendly meeting of the representatives of the new economic order and the most conservative exponents of the industrial countries, of the OECD countries. It was considered a major success that the Cancún conference did not take place in the hostile atmosphere that only a day before had been feared by President Reagan. There were friendly confrontations but what had been the object of the exercise? Surely, it was to get the discussion moving again, a discussion which had got into an impasse in the United Nations, on problems of development aid. Nothing like that happened. In truth I had not harboured great hopes.

It was said repeatedly yesterday that today we witness a crisis, and I would say the most serious crisis in history. Everything, but everything, seems to end up in paradoxical statements. For example, the World Bank which is supposed to control and stimulate the financial policy aspects of development or to participate in development ventures is as profitable as one of the biggest banks in the world. And the same holds for the International Monetary Fund. Both these banks which are supposed to help overcome the debt crisis as institutions make major profits, as you may have seen from the latest reports. Perhaps the people in charge are even proud that they have done such good business and that they have been so efficient. If on the other hand you know their activities as lenders, tying rigid and strict conditions to the granting of loans we can see that it is a situation of self-fulfilling prophecy. If we say that these credits will not be repaid either, these loans will not be repaid either—that is what I would like to venture to say—it is a self-fulfilling prophecy and

I am quite sure that once these fall mature they will not be repaid. We have seen what things have been happening in the developing countries. In spite of the fact that an improvement in the terms of trade had considerably improved their position, and their current accounts were greatly improved, at the same time their debt burden, their liabilities have increased much more rapidly than used to be the case.

To touch upon another paradoxical matter, the readiness of the rich countries has been reduced even more to live up to their obligations than used to be the case. We know full well that five years ago the situation of the developing countries was much better than it is today even though the necessity to bring about solutions stands out more and more clearly. But let me remind you—and I am fully aware of the fact that I am getting on people's nerves—let me remind you that some twenty years ago I developed a concept which I would like to put before you again. I tried to show that side-by-side with bilateral development aid, global multinational activities ought to be resorted to because the projects that have to be realised are too large to be coped with by individual countries, even the largest. My idea was that one should go back into the history of European economies and to see how these economies in Europe had developed. In so doing, as I looked as these things, I found that a great many of the things that had happened during the first half of the last century must be repeated with modifications; such as in Western Europe and subsequently in Eastern Europe, where an improvement of the infrastructure was brought about. In the same way, this must be done in the developing countries. Some of you may say, 'Well, of course', but a few years ago, when Servant Schreiber and a number of Japanese industrialists came to me—I was still Chancellor at that time—they told me that my ideas were wrong. They said that the developing countries ought to be immediately given the most advanced technologies; they should be spared the long and painful development of Europe. I think, in the case of the developing countries, it could be taken care of in one quarter of the time that was necessary for the development of Europe.

What are the most important essentials of infrastructure? First of all, there is transport. And here I think one has started the wrong way round. I should like to talk briefly about the renaissance of the railways. This is something we are witnessing also in Europe. Let me give you a simple figure: rail transport as compared with road transport is 1:5, as far as passengers are concerned. Why shouldn't one urge that in Africa a border-crossing railway network is developed? There are individual railway systems which are badly or not at all coordinated and therefore they are not in a position to work together. It is simply a question of coordination that ought to be set afoot. If we were able to do this we could, for example, stimulate a tremendous development of the resources of five African countries. And, of course, such a railway plan with all the geographical differences in question would help these countries greatly to develop their most important resources. I think that is a very important prerequisite. In addition, it would be necessary to have vocational training centres, vocational training schools in particular, in connection with the railways. Incidentally, I have found that amongst the leading proletarian forces in Eastern Europe, it was mostly the railway workers, railway mechanics, and so on, who took a leading role after the war within the communist parties and elsewhere.

A second example: Experience has shown that water management should be put on an entirely new basis in order that the water which is available can be used in an effective way, on the one hand for energy production and on the other hand for water management and water supply in the broader sense of the term. We know that, as far as water management is concerned, many new insights have been gained. In Israel, for example, they have had tremendous success, but it is not only in Israel but also in Gaddafi's Libya, a country which one does not like to refer to, generally speaking. If only a fraction of the effort that is often expended on meaningless criticism were spent on getting to know that country, perhaps one would see things differently.

An entirely new area in the field of infrastructure would be the development of telecommunications. This would include, again, occupational and vocational training centres. And what I believed would come about in the future has already become a reality; we have in Europe a tremendous surplus of teachers. Not only language teachers, Greek and Latin—ancient languages—not only a surplus of teachers of political science and sociology and the social services. We also have a great number of vocational training teachers who cannot hope for jobs in Europe and who would be urgently needed for infrastructural development in the Third World.

I could, of course, go on giving you examples. The Vienna Institute is currently undertaking a feasibility study concerning a particular railway project, and once all the details are known we shall try to find like-minded people and like-minded countries. And this model of what I am trying to develop here will then be presented to the public.

I am amongst the members of the older generation and I do remember what a tremendous impression the first successes of the first Five Year Plans made in the Soviet Union, and even made on people who did not sympathise with the Soviet Union and with communism. But, on the other hand, I also remember the tremendous project which was realised under the Roosevelt 'New Deal', the Tennessee Valley Authority project which, in its combination of energy production and the development of a region, had sensational consequences for the political thinking of a great many young people. A project which successfully works even today, even though it has been relegated to the background to a certain extent.

So what I would like to say here is that in my opinion we have a tremendous task before us. But as I say this, of course I am the lone one who cries in the desert; I am fully aware of that for whenever I visit State Chancelleries I have never found anything more than respectful attention. The institutions are there I think. The OECD ought to be in a position to realise such things. I am not a man given to delusions, I have a lot of practical experience and there is one more thing I would like to say on this. If one deals with the problem of permanent unemployment in the OECD countries—and I am not speaking of the unemployment problem in the developing countries—that is a monumental problem, a tremendous problem, but I do not dare even to touch upon it here. Some time ago the European Federation of Trade Unions—to which the Italian communist-dominated unions also belong (though not the French ones), and also the Christian trade unions belong, asked me whether I was ready to chair a commission similar to the Palme Commission and similar to the Brandt Commission, a commission to deal with the problem of unemployment. The important thing was that there should be no delegates from associations, rather this commission was to deal with the problem of permanent unemployment. Apparently they had selected me because I had for thirteen years chaired two commissions of the Social Partnership System, the mixed commission and the economic policy discussion round. As a small country, Austria has survived the crisis with a relatively low rate of unemployment. This summer we had an unemployment rate of about 3.5 per cent, and summer unemployment in Austria is the realistic figure I think. That is to say, it is a few fractions of a percent below the margin or near the margin that was called 'full employment' by Lord Beveridge, the inventor of that concept. I am mentioning this because I have come to be convinced that this type of unemployment, if it can be reduced at all—and please note that very cautious formula—it has to be fought by a multipronged attack. Prosperity as a panacea does not help. On the contrary, prosperity causes unemployment to grow because prosperity requires investments and the investments that are stimulated in this way are labour-saving investments, even though the factor of labour has long since lost its all-important role in the cost picture.

In this context I think one idea is particularly important, particularly in the democracies, and it is one that in my opinion that we ought to try: to tie the massive transfer of resources together with the problem of unemployment to make people more aware of the situation. This is quite contrary to the most honest and honourable efforts of our friends in the Netherlands and in Scandinavia not to do this: they say that one should not stress the utility for the donor-countries because that is immoral. But I say something different. I say that if we do not succeed in stimulating the self-interest of people in this matter, if we do not succeed in stimulating that self-interest, this is not a question that will be firmly anchored in the minds of men.

We know all that with the question of peace, that all of a sudden people came to be convinced that they themselves were directly threatened. For years and years, peace organisations close to the communist party had tried to convince people of the dangers of war, but it did not affect people except for a few fellow-travellers and a few well-meaning people. There were a few speeches made by representatives of today's American administration, such as the statement that 'An isolated nuclear war would be thinkable.' Just a few such statements gave so much momentum to the peace movement that even conservative prime ministers had to go to Washington and ask that the stationing of nuclear bases should be delayed because they had elections coming up or some similar reason. Even potential conservative voters all of a sudden were seen to be of a different opinion to that which their governments had advocated only a short time before. Today, it is not only the demonstrators in the streets who are aware of these dangers, there are in fact a great many others who are not ready to demonstrate in the streets but who nevertheless hold the same views. So, if we want to bring about genuine political awareness of the general public to the political questions we are discussing here, we will have to accept that we have got to tell them and we have got to make them understand that it is in their own self-interest that we make great efforts in this direction for the next ten or twenty years. It is certainly not the only way to fight unemployment, but it is one way to fight unemployment. And in my opinion it will help to reduce unemployment greatly because we create conditions in this way that these countries become new markets for the tremendous over-capacities at our disposal.

The American Under-Secretary of State, Lionel Olmer, made a speech in Austria last year in which he said that the fact alone that trade with the developing countries had been reduced had cost the American economy some thirty to forty thousand jobs. So, a country which had been greatly reluctant to go into these matters and which has not expended much money on such assistance is feeling the consequences. I am quite sure that we can help a lot if we make people aware of the fact that it is in their own interest to do something about this. And then the basic attitude that we find in the general public that this is a waste of money will finally give way to other—more realistic—considerations.

The media have not so far really clamoured for peace. Perhaps they reacted or they failed to react or they were hostile to this peace movement, but nevertheless the peace movement has become very strong despite the media, not with their help. And as long as tensions in the world persist, this question will arise again and again. We do not know whether so many new jobs will be created in this way as America maintains, but we do know that those that have found new jobs now have to be trained for these jobs, because the poor communities in the USA that have to finance primary schools do not get any grants from their federal government. And therefore the school leavers are inadequately trained for their jobs; that is to say, they have to be given follow-up training.

Partly then, a certain degree of illiteracy formation has taken place here. We do not know whether the wave of prosperity after the great crisis of unemployment of the 1930s, would actually have done away with unemployment fully, because we do know that it was already at that time that the war industry, the arms industry, was gradually started. And then, of course, unemployment was done away with when the United States embarked on the war. So when we deal with this problem there are a great many aspects that we have to take into consideration. And so, as I conclude my statement, I would like to say that we have not only to develop a new conception of how we can make the world aware of this. As I said yesterday in my introductory statement, Pandit Nehru once told me that it was not necessary to create a new Institute to give development assistance but rather it was important to have an Institute which would develop the philosophy and the theoretical basis for development aid, and where the practical basis of development aid were tested. But we all know how difficult that is. I would like to remind you of a concrete example which has always been fascinating to me, because I very soon got into contact with the people that counted in this particular instance. I am talking here of the Club of Rome. The Club of Rome had the great fortune to have a genius in the field of publicity in the person of Aurelio Paccei. What the Club of Rome said in its first few documents was not a secret to insiders but the documents of the Club of Rome have become burning issues in day-to-day politics; consider the issue of environmental protection, consider the concept of the finiteness of our resources. Whatever the Club of Rome dealt with at that time is now an indispensable part and parcel of government statements in all democratic countries.

And so I come to the conclusion that we ought to try to deal much more intensively with the question of how we have to rethink again the ideas for which we stand. That is why I have put the Vienna Declaration before you here which dates back to 1962 and was the product of two year's labours; my friend Ben Salah had a great part in this. I do believe that the most important thing today is to become clear in our minds what we actually want and then to reflect on how these things can be carried to the general public, how people can be made aware of this. This I think is the first and foremost question. I am not entirely sure whether this combination of development aid or cooperation can be tied into one parcel with the peace issue. If that could be done it would probably help a lot, because both these issues are of great topical importance. And the peace consciousness of people could be used as a vehicle making people aware of the fact that there is a potential danger of war also in the crisis that we are dealing with.

People are talking a great deal about the future and I recently quoted polemically a statement of Einstein. Einstein declared that he did not think about the future, which would come soon enough. And I said polemically that just because the future will arrive soon enough, we have got to deal with it now. And this question of cooperation between Third World countries and First World countries, this question is a question of particular importance for the future of us all.

I thank you.

Let Europe set the example

Louis Emmerij

May I congratulate at the outset of my address the Vienna Institute for Development through its President, Bruno Kreisky, and its Director, Arne Haselbach, as well as the management of *South* magazine on their initiative. Let me at the same time congratulate *South* magazine on the occasion of its fifth anniversary.

What a remarkable speech we have just heard coming from former Chancellor Kreisky about a plan which he has been pushing for so many years. I tend to agree very much with the proposal that there should be a stepped-up transfer of resources from the OECD countries to the developing countries. I also (and I am treated with less honour than Bruno Kreisky) get the same smiles of arrogance when people reply: 'But my dear Louis Emmerij, there is no political base for such a plan. Times are not ripe.'

Now, I for one, have never been very much impressed by the argument that at a given point in time there is no political base for an idea or for a policy suggestion. The last few years are an example of how fast the political base for pushing certain ideas can change. Unfortunately, for some of us the political base has changed—as has the political acceptability of ideas—in a direction which we do not altogether consider the right one. Only a few years ago we were talking about the post-industrial society. Now we are talking about re-industrialisation at any price. Only a few years ago—and Bruno Kreisky reminded us of that—we were talking about zero growth; now we are talking about economic growth at any price. A few years ago we were talking about a New International Economic Order, i.e. how to adjust the existing international order a tiny little bit to meet the needs of the poor countries. Today we are talking about how the poor countries must adjust to the needs of the existing international economic order. These are all illustrations of how fast the political base can change. What seemed to be absolutely impossible only a few years ago, has become the current orthodoxy in the financial, economic and social sphere of the day. In other words, I think one should test an idea on its relevance. Is a policy suggestion—like the massive transfer of resources— still relevant to meet the problems of the day? If the answer is 'no', forget it, and come up with a new idea. If the answer is 'yes', then we must prepare the ground in order for yet another orthodoxy in the financial and economic field to become the orthodoxy of the day in which these ideas are acceptable.

This is by way of introduction about the question of the political acceptability or the political base of an idea.

I would now like, Mr Chairman, to address myself to three issues. One is that of the changes that should take place in the OECD countries, mainly in the national decision-making process. There is not such a thing as an 'international decision-making process'; there are 160 'national decision-making processes', the sum total of which is something called an 'international order'. The debate about the rates of interest is an example, an illustration of how the national decision-making process in an important and respected OECD country can influence—disastrously I would add—the international scene, in this case the international debt situation. In the first instance, therefore, I shall speak about decisions that must be taken in the OECD countries. In this context, I shall react and elaborate upon some of the points made by Bruno Kreisky, namely the international stimulation of demand, or the need for a massive transfer of resources on the one hand, and the employment problem in the OECD countries on the other. Indeed, if we do not find an acceptable solution to the employment problem in the OECD countries, particularly in the European OECD countries—and by 'acceptable' I mean acceptable to employers and trade unions alike—there will be very little looking outward on the part of these countries and the political base for ideas, like a massive transfer of resources, will not be forthcoming. I would like to discuss these two elements at the beginning and follow them up with a third element, focusing more on the developing countries, but where decisions of international organisations and of rich countries are also of great importance; namely, the problem of adjustments in the developing countries and how to realise an adjustment policy with a human face, to use the expression of my friend and colleague, Richard Jolly.

First of all then may I react to, and elaborate on, the idea that European countries—I do think that the initiative should come from Europe—design and elaborate a programme to stimulate international demand, a variation of the Kreisky Plan.

I would like to distinguish here three groups of developing countries:

- the less developed countries;
- the middle-income countries; and
- the newly industrialising countries.

The transfer of resources should focus on the middle-income countries. All development cooperation efforts should concentrate on the low-income countries. And for the newly industrialising countries it is not the stepped-up transfer of resources, nor development cooperation, which is the main instrument of action. The main instrument for them, of course, is international trade, access to markets, etc.

The first point I would like to make, is that this 'Marshall Plan', this stepped-up transfer of resources, this stimulation of international demand, must be initiated by European countries, and be focused on the middle-income countries. Point two—the middle-income countries that are becoming members of that club should accept two conditions, and two conditions only: one is that the resources are being used for investment purposes and not for consumption purposes; the second is that they should be used for investments in certain sectors rather than in others. Again, agreeing with Bruno Kreisky, the resources should be used mainly for infrastructural works, in the industrial and agricultural sectors, but also to a certain extent for science and technology: for instance, solar energy research. It is remarkable to note that the bulk of research on solar energy is taking place in the industrialised countries, particularly in France and the Federal Republic of Germany, and that very little research in that field is taking place in the countries which would be the most important beneficiaries.

I would even go further and put a figure on such massive transfer of resources. I would have thought that the minimum amount of money that should be involved is US $20 billion a year for twenty years. Building up the infrastructure of countries is not something that happens overnight. We are talking about the package of US $400 billion between now and the end of the century.

Now, let me present some of the criticism that people advance with respect to such a plan. First, people will tell you that the absorptive capacity of the developing countries is too small. Well, I have heard that argument for a couple of decades. Twenty years ago it may have been true that the absorptive capacity of these countries was (too) small. But right now I am talking about the middle-income countries. And in these countries there has been remarkable progress, for example in the field of human resources and educational expansion. The absorptive capacity of these countries has become much bigger, and of course in a world where we have the kind of balance-of-payment deficits and the kind of international debts we face, to talk about the lack of absorptive capacity sounds to me as more than cynical. This is the first criticism I reject.

A second criticism is that it will endanger our own economies, and when I say our own economies, I mean the economies of the OECD countries. They will say: 'What! You are proposing to stimulate your own competitors? What naïvety!' Once more the naïvety is on the other side, because we know from empirical work that the industrialised countries have gained more employment opportunities by increased exports to the developing countries than they have lost by increased imports from the developing countries. The balance in all the countries where empirical work has been done—and it has been undertaken in practically all OECD countries—shows the same trends: the net balance is positive for the rich countries. And of course we know from other work in other fields that as countries move to the same level of development, the more international trade is taking place, the more it is to the mutual advantage of all these countries. So again, it is a criticism I must reject.

The third criticism was voiced more recently: 'How would such a plan have to be financed? In times like these, when the new financial and economic orthodoxy of the rich countries maintains that public expenditures must go down, and that the role of the state must become smaller, how do you dare to propose a plan that would precisely step up public expenditures of the rich countries?' In this case inadequate distinction is made between public expenditures that have a positive rate of return and public expenditures that have a zero or negative rate of return. Let me explain: much of the increase in public expenditures that we have noticed in recent years is due to the increased unemployment problem. Austria is blessed by the gods, or by Kreisky, because it had only a 3.5 per cent unemployment rate in the summer of 1985. It is an exception, and, by the way, an exception worth studying, because in the EEC countries the average rate of unemployment is 12.5 percent! And so we face the paradoxical situation that much of the increase in public expenditure has been caused by the increase in unemployment engendered in turn by the new orthodoxy in the financial and economic field. And that is a public expenditure on which for society at large there is a zero, or even negative, rate of return. By contrast, in the case of transfer of resources the increase in public expenditures will result in a positive rate of return in the shape of increased international trade. This criticism must therefore also be rejected.

Then there are those who say: 'But there was already a *private* transfer of resources in the 1970s.' That *is* true. The 1970s was the decade of the recycling of oil money through commercial banks from the North to the South. This line of criticism will go on to say that this increased private transfer of resources has created all the problems that we are now facing. The first reaction must be to say that this particular transfer has allowed quite a few developing countries to continue to grow during the 1970s. Second, at the end of the 1970s the banks started to impose variable rates of interest. Since then, of course, we know what happened: because of the national decision-taking of one important country these rates of interest varied alright, but in an explosive, upward direction. As of 1982 this resulted in the international debt problem, which in reality is an American rate of interest problem. This is one of the reasons why today we need a *public* stepped-up transfer of resources in order to counterbalance the problems countries now face through the private transfer of the 1970s. Once again, I am sceptical about that kind of criticism.

Finally—and as you see I am one of those people who defend an idea by giving a lot of credit to those who attack it—there is also a criticism to which I am more sensitive, and which argues that a massive transfer of resources maintains the unequal development pattern that many countries have been pursuing. In other words, isn't the status quo defended by your transfer programme, even if we are aware that it should also be changed?

We have Michael Manley here, who spoke yesterday. With persons like him in mind I would react to this kind of criticism by saying that we must use transfers of resources in order to help in particular those countries that are trying to change the status quo in the direction of a more acceptable development path, by paying more attention to the basic needs issue, for example. During such a transition period when you change from one development path to another, you necessarily run into trouble. You run into balance-of-payment problems, you run into financial deficits. These are the days when one needs one's friends, and it is precisely during those days that one finds one's friends are not there in sufficient numbers. On the whole countries are not stimulating you, they are hindering you. So, although I am sensitive to the last criticism, I, for one, would very much like to apply such a plan also to those middle-income countries that are undertaking delicate, but necessary, changes in their internal development policies.

So far for the stimulation of international demand. I am a partisan to that. In my opinion it is necessary and long overdue.

The second point in this presentation is about employment policy in the North, again a point mentioned by Bruno Kreisky. One cannot expect any enlightened international policy to come from the North if it cannot face the employment problem within its boundaries. It is clear—looking at the figures in some European countries like the UK, France, the Federal Republic of Germany as well as the Benelux countries, not to mention Spain or Ireland—that the employment problem will be with us at least for the next seven to ten years. I am not pessimistic about the longer term, but for the coming years—even with high rates of economic growth—we would not be able to tackle the employment problem without specific complementary employment policies. It is definitely not only economic growth that will do the trick, there must be something in addition. That is why the debate in many European countries which are not blessed by the gods revolves around reduction of working time. People are supposed to leave earlier, even if they do feel fit longer. It is the most fantastic destruction of human resources I have seen in a long time. Another method is to let people join the labour market at a later stage: the school must serve as a garage where the young are to be parked, so that they do not enter the labour market too early, a remarkable use of educational policy. Then there are those who are in favour of a thirty-two hours' or twenty-five hours' work-week, instead of the present forty to forty-two hours. Well, in our time we have seen several reductions of the working-week. My father used to work forty-eight hours a week, and then it became forty-five and in 1962 in my country it became forty hours. What did we see? Within five years technology had caught up and employment/unemployment were at the same levels as they had been before. So in fact there is a remarkable mythology going around in European countries about pseudo-solutions, dangerous solutions. The *Front Populaire* before the war has gone down the drain among others, because of premature reduction of working-time.

What I would like to propose is that during these seven to ten difficult years an all-out effort in investment in human resources is made. We are going through a period in Europe of important economic and technological restructuring. Moreover, before our own eyes we see arising a Europe of the transnational corporations. The European Industrial Round Table with twenty-three captains of industry was started by Volvo and Philips: Gyldenhammer (how does one pronounce these difficult Scandinavian names?) and Dekker (an easy Dutch name) together with Agnelli and others are the initiators. A Europe of the industrialists is now afoot, because the state is on the defensive, including the European 'state' in Brussels. Right now an all-out effort is taking place in European countries in the field of technology, in the face of the USA and Japan as well as some of the newly industrialising countries. We are witnessing the huge economic and technological restructuring of our societies. One cannot imagine such a restructuring taking place without a parallel restructuring of human beings, without investing not only in physical capital, but also in human capital. I, therefore, propose that the period of seven to ten years in Europe is being used for retraining, recycling people, taking them out of the labour market for longer consecutive periods of time in order to make them stronger and better equipped to (re)-enter the labour market afterwards. Is it not remarkable that in my country, the Netherlands, we are spending 25 billion guilders (that is a lot of money and with the dollar falling again, it is about 10 million dollars) to push people out of the labour market. Ten billion dollars on unemployment benefits, to make and keep people unhappy, with negative returns for society. Would it not be a much more intelligent policy to use that same amount of money not to push people out of the labour market, but to let a rotating group of people go out at specific intervals, voluntarily and temporarily in order to be retrained? That would be my suggestion to face the temporary employment problem in European countries today and to solve it in a multi-purpose and productive fashion.

I now come to the developing countries and to the question of adjustment policies, to the inter-relationship between policies in developing countries and policies in industrial countries and in international organisations. At the outset I must stress that the tendency of today to speak about the difficulties of the developing countries and that as a result of these development cooperation and development aid efforts have been a total loss is, again, a remarkable myth. The developing countries between the beginning of the 1950s and the end of the 1970s on average have grown by 5 per cent a year. Never have so many countries for such a long period of time grown at such a high rate in the economic history of the world. We must refute the myth that developing countries on average have done badly in terms of economic growth. It simply is not true. If you go back to the writings of the 1940s by the 'big shots' in the economic field, none of them expected and anticipated the rate of economic growth the developing countries have known. They were all extrapolating the trends of the industrialised countries over the last hundred years or so. The future tends to look like the past, even for the most intelligent people. If the past or the present is bad, the future will be bad; if the present is good, the future will be good ...! Two per cent per year, that was the anticipation for developing countries in the 1940s and 1950s. It turned out to be 5 per cent. Raymond Aron has talked about *les trente glorieuses* ('the thirty glorious years') when he referred to the industrialised countries. There is something like that taking place for the developing countries (and I am not being cynical). The real problem turned out to be the distribution problem, not the rate of economic growth.

I tried in the 1970s, when I was with the International Labour Organisation, to do something about that with the elaboration of the so-called 'basic needs' strategy. Today, something like a basic needs approach in developing countries is more relevant and more important than ever, in spite of or perhaps because of the trend to rely heavily on market forces.

Why do I say that? Just look at the kind of adjustment policies that are now being imposed. There are countries around this table—I am looking at Amir Jamal—that have been negotiating for five or six years with the World Bank and IMF. Look at the adjustment policies proposed by the World Bank and IMF. The way in which the poor countries are now being told to adjust to the needs of the current international order ensure that the poorest segments of their populations are hit hardest. There is very unequal burden-sharing nationally as well as internationally. Indeed, it is not only the developing countries that are responsible for the international debt situation. There is the responsibility of the rich countries, there is the responsibility of the commercial banks. I have been impressed by the lack of knowledge at the banks about the real problems of developing countries. They have gone into big lending transactions with the developing countries almost blindly. It is therefore a question of shared responsibilities and it would be unfair to require adjustments to be undertaken by the OECD countries, and above all by the USA, and by the private commercial banks. By the way, you are all undoubtedly aware that this year the USA has become an international debt country. It is now borrowing more money internationally than it is lending. It is borrowing to the tune of one hundred billion dollars a year. If that continues for only three consecutive years, the international debt of the USA will equal the Latin American debt of today and the USA would hardly qualify for an IMF loan!

Not only must there be international adjustment sharing, but also *within* countries the basic needs approach must be combined with the adjustment policies in order to make sure that minimum standards in the field of food, housing, clothing, education, health are being maintained while a country is in the adjustment stage. This is because what one observes when these adjustments are being imposed is that the decrease in public expenditure hits the 'soft' sectors like education and health most. Human resources development suffers most. At the moment these countries start to develop again, they will need precisely these resources most urgently. In other words, a short-term gain will be a long-term loss.

I would like to end by identifying two major choices that are confronting us today.

The first is whether we should continue with a global international division of labour, or whether we should move more into the direction of regional divisions of labour. Everything I have said so far, is based implicitly on a continuation of the global international division of labour, where everybody is dependent on everybody else, and sometimes to a remarkable and unhealthy degree. The possibility for a move towards several regional divisions of labour is not discussed. The interesting thing is, however, that one can see pointers that go into the direction of such a more regionally oriented division of labour in Europe rather than in developing countries. Some intellectual streams in developing countries have talked a lot about self-reliance and even de-linking. A move towards several regional divisions of labour is tantamount to more collective self-reliance. One can now observe the pointers of such an idea in Europe. For example, in the present financial and economic orthodoxy, there is a trend towards economic and technological restructuring of the European countries behind protectionist walls. Now, when I say 'protectionism' everybody says 'Wow!', but when I say 'collective self-reliance' everybody smiles. Yet, these are two sides of the same coin. Collective self-reliance necessarily means to an extent cutting oneself off from the rest of the world. This is a trend in the main stream of today's policies. One can observe it, secondly, in the 'Green' movements in Europe. They concentrate not only on a more environment-friendly and a more energy-extensive development pattern, they also stand for a more labour-intensive development pattern of European economies. A more employment-intensive development pattern necessarily means that your competitive edge is changing.

Thus, there are pointers that go into the direction of regional divisions of labour. They are not necessarily positive or positively intended, because in the case of the present European policies, for example, it means *reculer pour mieux sauter* ('withdraw and wait for a better opportunity for advance'). It means cutting ourselves off for a few years in order to gear up again, to put that huge economic machine on the rails again to reconquer the world market.

The second choice which has *not* been faced is the question of whether world economic recovery should occur sequentially or simultaneously. Today the implicit assumption is sequentially. We start with the United States, that is the locomotive, then comes Europe which is a smaller locomotive, and then the rest of the wagons, the convoy, will follow. However, it could very well be that the train is half-empty by the time the locomotives pick up speed again. I do not think that Africa, for example, could easily link on to that train. It may be left behind and that is why I am in favour—and the circle is now closed—of a simultaneous recovery which necessarily needs a stepped-up transfer of resources. I think the initiative should come from Europe. Europe is a world power in terms of population. It has a bigger population than the USA, or the Soviet Union, or, of course, Japan. Its regional product is the in order of US $2.5 trillion against US $3 trillion for the USA, the same order of magnitude. It has a bigger national product than the Soviet Union, bigger than Japan. Economically and demographically Europe is a superpower, politically it acts like a sheep, a *mouton*. It is time that Europe woke up, follows the gods that were born in Austria, and marches with its head held high towards a better destiny for the entire world.

Prospects for spaceship earth

Janez Stanovnik

You make my task, Mr Chairman, twice as difficult as I thought it would be. But don't expect too much and more particularly those of you who have already read my prepared statement should not be surprised that my statement is going to considerably depart from what I thought I would say when I left my country. For the changes the responsibility should be ascribed entirely to the preceding speakers who were so stimulating that I will just have to respond to their challenge than be content with the quiet thoughts I had when I left my country two days ago.

Permit me please, Mr Chairman, to spend a short time with more relaxed historical or almost philosophical thought. The roots, the philosophical roots of internationalism are very humanistic and very pacifistic and go back into the Middle Ages and the Renaissance. The first realisation, political realisation, of internationalism was colonialism and imperialism. It was the spread of this kind of internationalism here in Europe (more particularly in the Balkans) and in the rest of the world which led to the First World War, ending humanism and pacifism on the side of internationalism. After the First World War there was a short attempt to revive internationalism but the developments of the 1930s led us into the depth of economic nationalism and by the very logic of events this brought us into another bloody period of the Second World War which again confirmed the inhumane, aggressive and belligerent character of the practical implementation of economic nationalism. It is interesting that in the midst of the Second World War there were—I would say—romantic minds who started dreaming of World Government and were thus laying the ground of the post-war internationalism which was actually embodied in the creation of the United Nations and in the creation of the whole institutional family of the international organisations. I think that the background of this what I call romantic and utopian, Rooseveltian thinking, which was the basis of the concept of 'collective security', was guaranteed by the collective agreement of the Big Five powers. This romantic feeling and hope was brought down to earth very soon after the war and, similarly, the idea of gradually building up World Government through the IMF, the World Bank and the whole family of international organisations was very soon also confronted with a completely different kind of reality. Thus, we have from the very inception of the UN and of post-war internationalism this situation of—let me say—'facing the truth'. But despite a discrepancy between what was agreed and established in the UN Charter and the way events actually developed, it was the case that in these institutions there was a new political and societal reality which emerged after the Second World War.

Thus, we had the situation in the UN (and I am from now on mainly considering the economic developments) that in the Charter one could hardly find such words as 'development' or 'decolonisation'. Rather, it was such as the Trusteeship Council (a legacy of the mandate of the League of Nations) which was built into the Charter. As far as 'development' was concerned it was such concepts as 'stability', 'the common welfare', 'full employment' and such other niceties which were in the Charter, rather than 'economic development'. It may interest you to know—(I sometimes feel like a lexicon of the UN) that in 1947 the Stability and Employment Commission created a sub-committee for Economic Development, and the Indian delegate V. K. R. Virao dared to propose the same as Chancellor Kreisky explained to us this morning (namely, an agency to finance infrastructure which he called UNEDA); not only was his proposal rejected, but the sub-committee itself was dissolved. This was the state and spirit of affairs in 1947–48 in the United Nations. Now things have changed under the influence of new realities and new pressures which have come in. The Trusteeship Council was very soon an obsolete chamber; it was 'decolonisation', it was the declaration of the independence of colonial people which had taken the mind and which gave a new image and substance to the United Nations. It was U Thant's three 'Ds'—Decolonisation, Development, Disarmament—which were the three pillars of the United Nations and not the rhetoric which was put by the idealists into the Charter during the Second World War.

But this development has given rise to what I would like to call in hindsight what Stevenson called 'the liberal hour' in the UN and to the creation in the 1960s of UNCTAD and an entirely new development philosophy which placed development at the centre of international economic cooperation. All this has—as we can see from today's perspective—really brought about a very progressive development in human history. This, Mr Chairman, has actually brought us to two very substantial and basic historical achievements of UN: number one is 'decolonisation' which I think should not be considered only as a result—primarily, but not only—of the fight of the colonial people. It had also another element in it and this was that the new prevalent economic power—it happened to be the United States—wanted to have the world without borders, wanted to have free access; it was through this free access and the creation of world conditions for free access that the new power started developing what we call today 'transnational corporations'. These have given to internationalism a note of 'transnationalism' where suddenly the national entities (the nations whether ethnically conceived or juridically and state-like conceived as countries) have actually been diminished.

We have now arrived in a world where we still speak of internationalism but where the actual actors are no longer nations, no longer political and national authorities, but those who hold dominant power. There is, in my view, little point in entering into the argument as to how this came about historically and who is largely responsible for it. Somewhat—let me say—as a departure from the truth and from what is relevant, I find the Soviet argument that they have never been a colonial power, and that consequently they bear no moral responsibility for development aid both a departure from truth and irrelevant. I take the view of Burgh, the American historian, that we should draw a veil over whatever happened in the past. Let us rather look into where we are today and what we commonly and jointly can do today to make the world better.

It was this development—the progressive liberal development of the 1960s—which led us in the 1970s into a completely reverse situation. First, we suffered a unilateral re-shaping of the monetary system. Again, I prefer not to conduct an historical inquest into why the USA at a certain moment found it convenient to throw away a system which they themselves had built. It happened, and let us leave it at that. I consider that what followed, the 'oil shock', was a natural response to what came before. We should not argue now as to whether there was or was not an oil monopoly; the reality was that a market situation was created which was a natural monopoly. And it was only then the question of calling a spade a spade and to declare a monopoly what was in matter of fact a monopoly. Those who criticised the monopoly situation were the main consumers of energy who became so greedy for energy that they indulged in prodigious over-consumption in the situation of the time, a price rise was the most logical and natural thing for the producers to do.

However, this led to the inflationary and then deflationary situation of the 1970s throughout the developed countries with all its consequences.

If one reads the 1975 OECD economic outlook reports it is clearly stated that the most important immediate task for the developed world was not to permit the oil money to remain idle but to ensure that it must be recirculated, if the world was to avoid one of the worst depressions ever. Now, this advice of the OECD and the World Bank's advice (in the *World Development Reports* published in the late 1970s and the early 1980s) that prosperity was just around the corner, created an atmosphere of euphoria in which the South was seen to be flooded with money and debtors of yesterday had now become credit-worthy and were eager for the exports of the developed world. The South bears some of the responsibility for what followed for they had not appreciated the strings attached to the new prosperity. What has happened is that the former rule and domination of 'colonialism' has now been replaced by an indirect rule and indirect domination of concentrated economic power.

One could call this situation 'neo-colonialism', but I am not eager to indulge in name-calling; what I am concerned with is only to give an accurate description of the actual process which was under way, and the process under way is that of money. It is economic power which keeps the network and the machine working and operating. I am sorry to have to use such terms, but it is a situation of 'unequal exchanges'; you may call it 'exploitation'. This is the world we are actually in. Was this end-result the ingenious idea of those who engineered the debt strategy during the 1970s or was it accidental? I won't go into that. Whatever it was, the result is that the situation as it was created at the end of this period in the 1980s has blocked development, has actually created the situation where the developing countries, which had their own 'liberal hour' in the 1970s, were being suddenly pushed into one of the biggest, greatest depressions where economic development was almost completely blocked by the restrictive policies which have been imposed on them.

The main reasons for indebtedness, the main reasons also today for the debt crisis were external and not internal. There were and are tremendous difficulties and problems inside the developing countries. But, as this was rightly said by the preceding speakers, the amount of money which had been circulated by private banks is almost figure to figure identical with the amount of oil surplus which was deposited in Western private banks. And, again, this amount which was circulated in the world is almost identical to the level of the increase of Western exports to the developing countries, and the sum total of this amount is identical—and this is an essential point—is identical to the sum total of increases due to the increase of interest rates; to the loss of the terms of trade of developing countries, to the increase in oil prices, and, last but not least, to the loss in the volume of exports of developing countries. Accordingly, if you add up the figures—and it is not me who has done the exercise but the very respectable economist, William Klein, at the Institute of International Economics in Washington, accordingly a completely *zimmerrein* ('house-trained') person; it was he who has made this calculation and who has shown that the debt crisis is a crisis due to the external environment, to the changing circumstances in the world economy and not primarily to the failure of the internal policies of the developing countries. Developing countries had pursued wrong policies before and during this period, and will, no doubt, do so in the future as well. But these failures and these mistakes which have been made are not the core of the problem which the world faces today.

Thus, Mr Chairman, we have come into a situation, as I said, where we are confronted with basic problems. What are we going to do with the developing world which in 1985 has lost a full decade of economic development? The figures which indicate by any possible indication where the developing countries stand today, will show to you that they are below the indices of 1975. And if this trend continues, there will be no development because there cannot be development if you suppress imports. By suppressing the imports you deny yourself the foreign exchange content needed for investment. There is then a reverse flow of capital, at this moment amounting to more than 50 billion dollars a year. Perhaps, I should have said 'perverse' flow of capital, because today capital is not flowing from rich countries to poor, but from poor countries to rich countries. Under these circumstances the developing countries are transferring 4 per cent of their GNP, of their total production, for the interest payments alone, not to mention the principal. This means, that if they were growing by the rate of 4 per cent, they would just about be able to pay for their debts, and nothing else; they would still stand still. Now, the situation, tragic and dramatic as it is, requires from us an answer. What is the answer? When you read any economic survey, whether produced by the World Bank or by the Monetary Fund or by OECD or by the Bank for International Settlement they all use marvellous models. Now, the gist of those models are various export elasticities, import elasticities; all the niceties that are produced by modern-day econometrics. However, they are all built on one assumption, and this assumption is that there is no way for the developing world but from the traditional links between North and South. None of these models work. However you manipulate the figures you never come out with a positive result. Now, therefore, for me the question is that we cannot hope to get anything by just hoping that the Good Lord is on the side of the poor, and that He will once again demonstrate our historical justification that He always helps the poor and finally He will this time. I would rather not advise anybody to be so religiously devout in the face of the historical evidence. Rather that if we are truthful to ourselves and to the developing countries, then we must face them with the truth.

I would like to conclude with seven points of advice or recommendations which emerge from my own reflections on this problem; they are largely in line with what other speakers have suggested.

Number one, and I attach most importance to this, is that the development pattern must be changed. Unless something is done inside the developing countries there is no hope. We have had so far various theories. After the war, I was at that time a young man full of enthusiasm for Harold Domar's theory of capital output ratios, and Summitro's theories where one just put more capital in and one got more output out; that was the whole secret, and therefore we have been all for investment, investment, investment.

Now historical experience has shown that this model very soon failed. And I don't have time now to go into why it failed. We have then after that (after we have been desperate all on this what I call GDP-target and targetting) the period of so-called international development. Development should be international, but it was not long before the transnationals taught us a lesson; that international development would introduce the transnational corporations. The experience of transnational development in Chile and other countries, made us realise that this is not the kind of development that people actually wanted. Then we were trying to get yet another formula, and we came during the UNCTAD years upon the formula of 'growth through trade'. I was also one of those who was encouraging 'growth through trade' during the trade gap of Prebisch's time. Now, what has happened? The 1970s and 1980s have come and they have taught us a lesson; we have suddenly realised what it means if the countries become in their historical development, in the fate of their economic development, completely dependent on a completely unpredictable international environment. We see that it is not one's domestic motivations, it is not the conditions of one's own society which decides the fate and destiny of one's nation, it is decided by random events elsewhere and it just comes and is bestowed upon you.

So we have been taught one by one a lesson of these various attempts which we have made, and none of them has actually worked. I have no better advice but 'Follow your own way'. What does this mean? There is only one, only one being in the whole creation which has the capacity to create, and that is the human being with work. Therefore, I think that the most precious reserve or resource which we have are people. In all developmental thinking so far we thought in terms of GNPs, in terms of investment, in terms of productivity and all kinds of niceties, but we have not really been thinking enough in terms of people. We have been talking of basic needs but basic needs still were development for the people. What we need today is also Jeffersonian development of the people and the development by the people. It is in my view this complex which gives us then in the development process the totality and, in a way, almost an identity with the totality of the democratic process. Human rights are not irrelevant in the consideration of economic development. Without human rights we cannot control demographic trends. Only if we will have human rights, which includes the rights of women, then we will have under control also the demographic trends, then we will have the kind of economy which I think could again lead us back on the rails of economic development. This in my view is prerequisite number one.

Prerequisite number two which comes directly from the hard history of the 1980s is 'collective self-reliance'. I am very sorry, Louis, because I find myself always enthusiastically in agreement with whatever Louis Emmerij says. But when this morning he was making a hardly hidden link between collective self-reliance and protectionism, I say 'No, Louis, this not so!' Why not? You possibly cannot say if I am attacked by a machine gun and I grab a stick, that I am the same kind of brigand as the one who attacked me. It is one thing to attack, another thing to defend oneself. You cannot possibly say that to me if I am calling for collective self-reliance, for greater links among the Southern people, for South–South economic cooperation after the developed world has built up all the possible walls of their own inward lookingness. The sugar planter or the sugar-grower in the European Community gets three times the world market price of sugar. This is a little bit too much for me. I consider that collective self-reliance is the only way to bring this world back to some kind of balance. We cannot have a real world economy, which will be only North–South, unless the South builds its own basis in the economic, financial and other areas. We will never be talking to each other as equals if the South will not have its own basis. Therefore I consider the South–South relationship is absolutely indispensable if we want to return to what I would call a sound world economy.

Now the third point would be 'the new alliances'. Tindbergen likes to talk about 'the new alliances' and the Club of Rome has published much on this. I think there is something in this. During our symposium there has been talk of the 'neutrals' and the 'non-aligned'. Here in the European area it works very well. I think that the European Security and Cooperation Conference would never have achieved the results it did were it not for this reliance between the neutrals and the non-aligned. But we must go beyond that. I consider that the Greenpeace group, whether they clash with President Mitterrand or not, they are in Europe a real force. However, they are concerned primarily with European affairs, and they do not see beyond the divide to the South. I consider that this potential force and power should be brought into what today is actually the main requirement of civilization. If we do not resolve the problem of Southern development world civilization will go down the drain. This must be properly understood. I consider therefore that on the political ground we should be working for new alliances, and therefore not only exerting Southern pressure on the North, but also mobilising inside the North the progressive and positive forces which will help in the solution of what I consider to be a problem of civilization.

My fourth point concerns the UN. It is today the fortieth anniversary of UN. It is largely forgotten that the Charter opens with the words 'We, the

Peoples of the United Nations'. It doesn't say, as did the Covenant of the League of Nations, 'We, the High Contracting Parties'. No, the UN is not composed of states, the UN is composed of people, but in the past it was forgotten that the UN is of people. I consider that this element of UN—that is, as not only representing the states and being a diplomatic forum, but being a forum for people and speaking out of concern for civilization, this element is, in my view, tremendously important.

My fifth point is about the reform of the financial system. I am sorry that on this matter I cannot entirely agree with Teresa Hayter. My experience was different. I still see Eugene Black in front of us in the Security Council and speaking as loudly and as unequivocally as he could. He said: 'Quasi-loans— never.' Now then IDA came, and IDA was accepted. IDA was a tremendous developmental institution in UN. And if I am critical today—not on the same ground as you are, of the Bank—it is because IDA is under pressure. This most important developmental institution in the international system is today under pressure.

Now for for the IMF; I am a foremost critic of IMF, having just recently published a whole book on the topic, but I cannot deny the fact that Schweitzer has introduced the SDR, and that SDR has had tremendous capacity to transform the IMF into a genuinely developmental institution. Equally, I consider Witteveen's actions in the course of the oil crisis, with the supplementary financing programme has also made a very marked attempt towards making the IMF a developmental institution.

My sixth point is that I consider that trade and the trade system requires a change as well. Now, in the trade system, unlike the discussion is going on today in the GATT, I consider the basic problem is actually the problem of the further course of industrialisation. Trade, for me, should be spoken in Vienna at UNIDO and not at GATT. Further, it should be a joint discussion of trade and finance. There is no case whatsoever for the bankers pressing to get their high-interest money back and then the traders hiding themselves behind a protectionist wall. This way the world will just go on going down, and we will never emerge from the difficulties we are in.

My very last and seventh point is that we should all understand (and I am sure that Mansour Khalid as a Vice-Chairman of the World Commission on Environment and Development, will welcome what I say), that we should all learn to live with what Kenneth Boulding has called a 'spaceship economy'. We are living on a spaceship economy. If the Mexican earthquake has not reminded you that the earth may anywhere shake beneath your feet, that we are actually living on a very precarious biological ground; if you do not realise that, then please open Olof Palme's report, and you will see what a 'nuclear night' could mean to mankind. And it is not so far away; everyone of you around this table and your children and everybody in the world has today over his head twenty tons of trinitro-tuluol explosive, and we are carrying it around the world. This is the precarious aspect of our survival. If we do not understand that and we still stick to our sovereignties, to our small little gardens and do not understand what at least here in this area of wars we did not understand (if not today, then certainly in the past) that *Ex pluribus unum* ('One out of many'). Among all our differences we should understand that we are all human. And if we do not behave as human beings to each other—and I have just attended a panel on South Africa—if we don't understand that we are all from one human family then we will be morally corroded to the extent that we will be unable to survive.

Thank you.

Is reform of the World Bank possible?

Teresa Hayter

I should like to make my view of the World Bank clear at the outset, and then attempt to substantiate it. It is, first, that the World Bank is basically an instrument of the foreign economic policies of the United States and its major Western allies. As such, the Bank's overriding objective is the preservation of the capitalist system in the Third World, or, as one of its more frank officials put it, the promotion of 'capitalist efficiency'. Since many of you have no objections to such a goal, I should add that my own position, which I shall not try to substantiate here, is that capitalism in the Third World is incompatible with the interests of the poor.

Secondly, I believe it is possible to go further. The World Bank, while it may or may not itself be efficient in its promotion of 'capitalist efficiency', whatever that means, does, I believe, give preference to the interests of capitalism in the major Western powers over those of capitalism in the Third World.

Third, it is clear that this will not change unless there are radical changes in the governments of major Western powers, including of necessity the government of the USA. I think it is possible to make similar, but not identical, assertions about the IMF and the other multilateral development banks (MDBs), although I shall not attempt to do so now.

One of the clearest demonstrations of the nature of the World Bank's allegiances is to be found in its public behaviour over the debt crisis of the early 1980s. The World Bank is effectively part of the lenders' cartel which confronts the debtor countries. The purpose of this cartel is to ensure that the burden of the crisis falls, not on the banks or the taxpayers of the creditor countries, but on the debtor countries. The debt crisis was largely not of the debtors' making; it was the result of the economic problems of the major capitalist countries and their response to them. Moreover, because of the particular form taken by the austerity programmes imposed through the agency of the IMF as a condition of debt rescheduling, the burden of sacrifice has fallen most heavily on the poor in those countries.

The World Bank's loans have sometimes been part of the so-called 'rescue packages' worked out between the IMF, the private banks and government; the World Bank usually does not lend to goverments which fail to reach agreement with the IMF. Moreover, its public statements have been confined to stern warnings against default, together with exhortations against protectionism in the developed countries. Apart from one statement by Clausen, early in 1984, shortly after the US cut in IDA replenishment, that the current net transfer of capital out of the Third World was 'premature' on this scale, there has been no indication that I am aware of that the Bank's senior management consider that excessive demands are being made for governments to cut imports and accumulate trade surpluses in order to service their debts at the current exorbitant rates of interest. In its demands for strict adherence to contractual obligations for debts, the World Bank is being true to long-standing traditions; its first loans in Latin America, to Chile, were made only after that country had reached accommodation on its pre-war debts with the US Foreign Bondholders Protective Council Inc. and the Council of Foreign Bondholders of Great Britain, among others. But Clausen himself, the latest in a line of banking Presidents, does appear to have particular enthusiasm for what he has called 'a new era of partnership between the World Bank and international commercial banks for helping the economies of the developing countries'. One of his few claims to innovation has been the introduction of new 'co-financing' instruments, designed to link World Bank lending more closely with that of the private banks.

The other major constant throughout the Bank's history has been its support for foreign private investment. The recommendation that more reliance should be placed on it has been one of the Bank's unvarying, stock recommendations in all of its reports, and I have never discovered any questioning of its virtues. The Bank's response to requests for loans to finance industry in the public sector is normally to ask why the project cannot be in the private sector, which effectively, in most cases, means the foreign private sector. The Bank at times gets accused by its right-wing critics, and claims to its left-wing critics, that it supports the public sector, since its loans must be made to governments or with government guarantee. But, until the Bank began in the 1970s to increase its lending for agriculture, its loans were overwhelmingly in the economic infrastructure. As a US Treasury Report, commissioned by the Reagan Administration apparently to investigate whether the Bank supported 'socialism', concluded: 'available evidence on MDB lending does not support the conclusion that MDBs have sought to support the public sector at the expense of the private sector'; moreover an overwhelming proportion of Bank lending is for projects which would be in the public sector or publicly regulated in the USA and 'such lending can in fact indirectly promote the private sector by providing services essential to its development'.

India and Algeria are notable examples of countries which have fought protracted battles with the Bank on the question of whether projects should be in the public sector, or financed by foreign private investment. Algeria, having failed to get any support from the Bank, built up its state oil and gas industry by borrowing from private commercial sources, without recourse to the oil companies. In India the Bank finally, in the 1970s, dropped its refusal to lend to fertiliser projects in the public sector; an Indian official suggested that this was because the foreign fertiliser companies were no longer interested. The Bank has also lent on a considerable scale, and for a time it appears against US opposition, to the Indian Oil and Natural Gas Company; but by 1983 it was telling the ONGC 'not to embarrass us by asking for more'; it also attempted to persuade the Indian government to offer areas with proven reserves to the oil companies.

In general, Clausen, US government officials and the US Treasury Report all use identical language in describing the principal role of the World Bank: it is to act 'as a catalyst for flows of private capital'. Bank officials nevertheless claim that the fact that they favour such flows has nothing to do with ideology; it is merely a matter of 'efficiency'. Eugene Black, setting the tone in the early days of the Bank, said: 'What government does not have its hands full without reaching out into new fields? What government has so much foreign exchange that it can afford to bar a responsible foreign investor? There is no ideological argument here. Just common sense.'

The Bank has in fact had a curious ability to make the notion that it is politically impartial stick. This is perhaps partly because, until recently, it has been notably secretive about its attempts to influence the economic policies of its borrowers, except at the level of projects. Some Bank officials still appear to believe, no doubt correctly, that if the full extent of the Bank's attempt to influence general policies were more fully known, then the Bank would lose its relative immunity from criticism; IMF riots would become known, as they ought to be, as 'IMF/World Bank riots'. Nevertheless, Bank documents and Clausen speeches now openly proclaim that the Bank's euphemistically-termed 'policy dialogue' is as important as its funding of projects. They still tend to be rather unspecific on what the dialogue is about.

The result is that probably many people still would not accept that the demands made by the Bank differ remarkably little from the demands made by the IMF. The conflicts between them that might be expected to result from the fact that the Fund is officially concerned with short-term stabilisation, whereas the Bank is supposed to be concerned with long-term growth, have been neatly resolved by the Bank's explicit acceptance of the Fund's contention that its austerity programmes are a precondition of growth. The

Bank's programmes contain the same stock list of recommendations as the IMF's do: cuts in public expenditure and credit expansion; reductions in controls on prices, imports and movements of capital; reduction or elimination of subsidies; wage cuts; devaluation; 'reform' of the public sector (which means making it smaller); greater reliance on market forces and the private sector; and so on. It is true that the World Bank is recognised as having specific responsibilities for advising on the government's investment programme. But this is in the context of cuts. There is no evidence that the Bank is in any general way a more expansionist institution that the IMF. Bank officials are unable, or unwilling, to supply any evidence that the Bank contests the ceilings imposed by the Fund. It is possible that they have done so, on occasion; but it is equally possible that there have been circumstances in which the Bank has favoured a harsher policy than the IMF. During the period, in the late 1970s, of greater Fund 'flexibility', the Bank was one of its sterner critics; an IMF official relates how, summoned to a meeting with country economists in the Bank, he embarked on a defence of Fund stabilisation policies; he was told he was 'setting up a straw man'; on the contrary, the IMF should be more rigorous; it was 'pulling the rug from under our (the Bank's) feet'.

There is also no evidence that during the period of McNamara (which in retrospect seems like a golden age!) the Bank changed the nature of its general advice to governments. In my recent research, I asked Bank officials fairly systematically what pressures they had been putting on governments to do more for the welfare of the poor, to redistribute wealth, and so on. The only claim that was made in this respect was in the case of Brazil. It turned out that the Bank has in fact put pressure on Brazil, but that the pressure took the form of demanding that Brazil should undertake a rural development *project*. My belief is that the Bank's 'poverty orientation', such as it was, was entirely confined to projects. As for the projects themselves, there is much that could be said. The most important fact is that the projects represent some 2 per cent of total investment in the Third World; of that 2 per cent, less than a third was for projects in agriculture and less than 15 per cent was for other projects related to poverty issues, such as water supply and housing. In the latter case, the Bank was hampered by its adherence to the neo-classical principle of full cost recovery. The Bank finds it hard to deal with the very poor for the simple reason that they have no money. Somewhat the same applies to the Bank's projects in agriculture, with the additional consideration that the Bank actively believes in encouraging so-called 'progressive' farmers, the farmers who already have some assets, and who are supposed to provide an example to the ignorant poor. In addition, there is much evidence that even supposing the Bank was fully committed to ensuring that the benefits of its projects went to the poorest, the compulsion to lend is such that proper supervision is viritually impossible.

Probably the clearest evidence that the Bank, in spite of its repeated claims to the contrary, is not in fact politically impartial, is that it has a long history of refusing to lend to left-wing, or merely reformist, governments. This began in the 1950s with refusals to lend to Poland and Czechoslovakia. The Bank did not lend to Chile under Allende. It did not lend to Grenada under Maurice Bishop. It stopped lending to Nicaragua in 1982. It has not lent to Vietnam since the liberation of the South. It did not lend to Algeria for the first ten years after its independence. It stopped lending to Peru during the period of reformist military government. It stopped lending to Jamaica under Manley, to Brazil under Goulart, to Egypt under Nasser. And so on. Invariably the Bank claims technical reasons for its refusals to lend. Thus in Algeria it cooked the figures to make the projected rate of return on an irrigation project look low by insisting on including the capital cost of a dam previously built by the French. In Grenada, rising above the fact that the Bank has previously itself produced a report favourable to the Point Salinas airport project, it claimed that the project was unsound and used this as a reason to state that the government's investment programme as a whole was unsound and the Bank therefore could not lend (and nor should others).

Sometimes the Bank says that a government's programme is 'internally inconsistent', that governments 'cannot just hand out to everybody'. True though this is, it is clear which handouts the Bank is against, and those are not the handouts to the rich. In the early years after the Sandinistas' victory, a leaked Bank Country Consultative Paper argued for a continuation of Bank lending, but at a reduced rate, on straight political grounds: the economy was 'in flux' and there was some possibility that a continued Bank presence would ensure a greater orientation to the private sector. But even this policy was quickly abandoned; a Bank official said the Bank's decision to stop lending was based on the departure of some technocrats willing to talk to the Bank; US pressures no doubt also played their part. Sometimes it is said that the Bank is happier with established left-wing governments. Happy or not, there is clearly little that the Bank could do to de-stabilise Hungary or China by threatening not to lend to them; but, by lending, it explicitly hopes to push these countries along the road to 'market-orientated' policies. Asked whether the Bank had ever stopped lending to a right-wing government on the grounds of inefficiency, a Bank official in 1981 said: 'Zaire'. But this stand was short-lived. There are on the other hand numerous right-wing governments, including for example those of Turkey and Egypt, to whom the Bank has lent during periods when their economies were clearly, according to Bank officials themselves, 'in a mess'. The Bank was moreover induced by US pressures, shortly before the liberation of Saigon, to organise a consortium of donors to provide aid to the Saigon regime; and it is currently under pressure to lend to El Salvador.

Supposing it is accepted that the Bank favours capitalism rather than socialism in the Third World, are there other more specific ways in which the Bank favours the interests of the West? As I have already said, the Bank's President and senior management, though not all of its officials, are clearly happy to do what they can as debt collectors for the West, whatever the justice or injustice of the creditors' case. As I have also said, the Bank vigorously promotes private investment from the West, including in cases where this is in conflict with the public and even the private sector in the Third World. This has been, notably, the case in the oil industry, where the Bank has normally made loans for (risky) exploration and left the (safe) exploitation of the discovered reserves to the oil companies (perhaps as a direct result of US pressures). In addition, the Bank is notorious for promoting the import of manufactured goods rather than the establishment of local industries. It does so, of course, on the stated grounds that foreign manufacturers are more 'efficient'. It backs up its argument by recourse to the hoary old weapon of the industrially strong: the theory of comparative advantage. This argument has allowed the Bank to tell just about every country that proposed to build a steel mill, not to do so. It enabled the Bank to tell Pakistan (before its division) not to process jute and South Korea not to build ships. No doubt the Bank told Japan in the 1960s not to build motor cars. And the urgings continue. When the Algerian government asked for a loan to establish an industry to build fishing boats, the Bank proposed a loan to import them from abroad. When the Indian railways needed computers, the Bank fought long battles with Indian government departments to persuade them that the computer system should be imported ready-made, rather than developed locally. Usually there are good arguments on both sides in such questions; but it is always obvious which side the Bank will be on.

The Bank insists on 'international competitive bidding' for the projects it finances. The 15 per cent so-called 'preference' which it accords to local suppliers is a substitute for, not an addition to, the country's own tariffs, and was introduced because the Bank's shareholders considered that these were excessive. The Bank normally determines the choice of consultants, whose cost, incidentally, forms a high proportion of its projects' costs; once the consultants have been chosen, it is fairly clear who the suppliers will be. The Bank has been accused, not often of corruption, but of designing projects in such a way that only or mainly Western contractors will be suitable to bid for them.

The Bank has been at least as committed as the IMF to the goal of import liberalisation. In the Philippines and Peru, and no doubt elsewhere, it has had a more direct and successful role in promoting this goal than the IMF. The Bank has long argued that the secret of export promotion is import liberalisation. Its research activities in this field, curiously at a time of mounting protectionism in the West, have recently been intensified. While its view of comparative advantage has shifted, though not consistently through-out the world, to the view that cheap and repressed labour is a component of comparative advantage in many Third World countries, which may now aspire to export light manufactured goods as well as primary commodities and raw materials, the Bank remains opposed to attempts to set up heavy and intermediate industries. This is the case even, for example, in a country as large as Brazil. And the Bank is of course opposed to their protection. It is difficult to determine whether the Bank is motivated by blinkered adherence to neo-classical (and of course time-serving) theory, or whether it consciously sets out to serve the interests of established industry in the West. But the effect is the same.

The possibilities of reforming such an institution are constrained by the fact that its structure and ownership are different from those of other UN institutions. The Bank is dependent on raising money in private capital markets. Its voting structure is such that the USA and five other major subscribers have a potential voting majority on its Board. In cases where the USA is still not confident of a majority, the nature of the Bank's Presidents and staff, their autonomy, the hierarchy of their relationships, their location in Washington, all facilitate direct pressures from US officials to ensure, for example, that loans which the USA does not want made do not get submitted to the Board, (and that others do). The Bank has nevertheless found it difficult to get funds for IDA from the current US Administration. This is in spite of an almost wholly favourable US Treasury report commissioned by the Reagan Administration, which concluded, among other things, that the 'recipients' perception of (the Bank's) impartiality' made it 'better placed to advise LDCs of the benefits of an international system based on trade and capital flows and to elicit market directed changes in recipients' economic policies'. And in spite also of Clausen's attempts to make the Bank's rhetoric conform to its reality: 'One of my main management objectives,' he told the *Financial Times*, 'is to make the perception of what the Bank does closer to what it actually does.' It seems that too many people had taken McNamara's eloquence at face value; the Bank has become tarred, in the eyes of Congress and Reaganites at least, with the brush of socialism; and IDA got its funds cut. If the Bank's reality did in fact conform to its rhetoric, it is doubtful whether it would get any money at all.

It may be said that other US Administrations have been different and might be so in the future. But it is not likely that their view of the essential foreign policy interests of the United States will diverge sharply from those of the Reagan Administration. Would President Carter not have tried to organise a credit and trade boycott of Nicaragua or of the Popular Revolutionary Government in Grenada? The history of the World Bank demonstrates that it could not for long act against what the US government considered were its interests—even supposing its staff and mostly banking Presidents wished to do so—and get IDA replenished.

The British Labour Party's hope that, by supporting the Bank, it can 'support the progressive policies which (the World Bank) has been developing, and also encourage it to support forms of socialist organisation where these can make a visible economic contribution to Third World development', remains pie in the sky.

Conclusion

Thorvald Stoltenberg

I will try to give the summing up which is a fairly difficult task. You will all realise that either I had to prepare this summing-up before I heard the speeches, or I had to do so during the speeches. I have tried to do both.

The purpose of this meeting is to try to contribute to getting things moving again and it may be a paradox for the Chairman to say that this meeting is more important than it should be. I say this, however, because I think that 'getting things moving' should be the task of governments and, with very few exceptions, we here are all out of government. However, we as a group, are one of the very few groups who can really push to try to get things moving again. I have summed up our two days' deliberations under seven points and I have called my seven points the 'Vienna Way'. I have tried to abstract from the various speeches what can be indicative of concrete action, what can we put in our pocket as a memorandum from this meeting to bring up at the next meeting we attend, abroad or at home in order to push things to move again. Let me briefly give you the seven points; I do so briefly because all of these points have been deliberated upon by many or most of the speakers.

First, common interests: the importance of the full recognition both in North and South of common interests, not only in the long term but also in the short term. And the code words would be economics, employment, security.

Second, economic and social development as a means of strengthening democracy and vice versa, or to put it even more succinctly, as Stanovnik did, development for the people, of the people and by the people.

Thirdly, strengthening people-to-people cooperation across borders. The proletariat were the first to join, to unite across national borders but the transnational corporations have also done it. I think it is high time to see how cooperative developments with trade unions, women's movements, non-governmental organisations, human rights movements can be intensified across national boundaries. This is the best way to promote democracy and human rights, much better than pressure from one government to another, which often works the opposite way.

Fourthly, the revival of multilateralism and the strengthening of international organisations; as a symbol of this we should look particularly to the United Nations. And I hope most of you have read or will read Marc Nerfin's article—it is distributed at this meeting—with its ideas how the UN can be revitalised. This is first and foremost a political task; we have had enough commissions, enough studies, it is now a political issue as to how to create support for reforms of the UN and the system of international institutions in general. This should be particularly the task of the South and the small and medium-sized countries. These are the countries who will have a direct interest in strengthening multilateralism. Under this point I also include reform of the IMF and the World Bank.

Fifth, yesterday I think all the speakers referred to the need for initiatives and cooperation between the South and 'like-minded' countries. I am pleased to tell you that this is not just theory, it is actually practised today in the sense that the four Scandinavian governments have entered into negotiations with the Southern countries, the Front Line States, on what is symbolically called 'Mini New Economic Order'. It is more than an aid package. How much more shall we put into it? Banking, finance, currency, commodities, trade, technology, no one knows. But these negotiations are currently going on which is a typical example of South-'like-minded' cooperation to move things, to push things forward.

Sixth, strengthening the South, through South–South cooperation, and the creation of a South secretariat. I think most of the speakers have stressed the need for South–South cooperation. Some have even put South–South cooperation as something as a demand towards the North. Since I am the last speaker I will be rude. Stop talking about South–South cooperation, do it! It is up to the South to do it, to get things done. We should not any longer delay.

And now the seventh point, the massive transfer of resources. I know that many people believe that a massive transfer of resources is not realistic. But those who doubt that I will remind you that in 1979 we were close to a planned massive transfer of resources. It is possible. We just have to not give up and to push these ideas.

These are the seven points which I ask you to take home and promote as practical, concrete-oriented actions that we can and should take as a result of this meeting and many other meetings. This is how we can influence international development. We many be criticised, for being too ambitious in the North–South context. My answer always is that I could give a much longer, better and more logical speech showing how this world may collapse into chaos and violence. But I do not see any point in that. I think the reason why we come together is to see how we can improve the conditions and how we can find solutions to the problems we are faced with. Our main task is to try to contribute to bringing the present North–South situation out of deadlock.

NOTES ON CONTRIBUTORS

Louis Emmerij

Rector, Institute of Social Studies, The Hague, since 1976. From 1st January 1986, President of the OECD Development Centre, Paris.

Born in Rotterdam 1934. Educated at University of Paris, Johns Hopkins University and Columbia University.

Dr Emmerij has worked at the OECD Directorate of Scientific Affairs, 1962–1970, and as Director, World Employment Programme, ILO, 1971–76, where he was responsible for developing the ILO basic needs approach. He was appointed Rector of the Institute of Social Studies at The Hague in 1976.

Dr Emmerij was President of the European Association of Development Research and Training Institutes (EADI), 1978–84, and is a member of the Governing Council of the Society for International Development (SID).

He has worked in Yugoslavia, Argentina, Sri Lanka, Kenya, The Cameroon and has published numerous books and articles on education, labour markets, economic and development issues. He is the co-author of 'From the Old to a New Global Order: A Consistent Survival Strategy' (1979).

Altaf Gauhar

Editor-in-Chief of 'South—The Third World Magazine' and of the *Third World Quarterly*; Secretary-General of the Third World Foundation.

Born in Gujranwala 1923. Educated at Government College, Lahore, Pakistan.

Altaf Gauhar was a member of the Pakistan Civil Service from 1946 to 1970 and held the following offices: First Secretary of the State Bank of Pakistan; Chief Controller of Imports and Exports; Finance Secretary of West Pakistan and Permanent Secretary to the Ministry of Information and Broadcasting. He was the founder of Pakistan Television Corporation and was its first Chairman. He was leader of the Pakistani delegation to the GATT Conference in 1961 and to the Cairo Non-Aligned Economic Conference in 1962.

From 1971 to 1973 he was Editor-in-Chief of the DAWN group of newspapers and was twice detained as a political prisoner. He moved to the United Kingdom in 1976 and helped in the setting up of the Third World Group. He was the Co-Editor of the Guardian Third World Review and in that capacity received the British Press Award (1978).

He is life Vice-President of the International Federation of Modern Languages and Literature (FIMLL).

His publications include: *Translations from the Quran* (1974); *The Challenge of Islam* (1977); *Free Flow of Information; Islamic Concept of Economic Order; Talking About Development* (1983); *Third World Strategy* (1983); *The Rich and the Poor*, (1983); *Regional Integration: The Latin American Experience* (1985) and *Shared Horizon* (1985).

Humayun Gauhar

President and Publisher of *South* magazine, Managing Director, Third World Foundation since 1980.

Born in Karachi, Pakistan 1949. Educated at the University of Punjab and at the University of Cambridge.

Prior to publishing *South* magazine Mr Gauhar was Chairman of Micas Associates Ltd., a management and turn-key consultancy organisation as well as Chairman of Micas Food Industries Ltd., Pakistan. He was also actively involved in national politics in Pakistan.

Teresa Hayter

Research Editor for the Greater London Council's (GLC) London Industrial Strategy and other GLC publications.

Ms Hayter was attached to Oxford Polytechnic and was given a British Social Science Research Council (SSRC) research grant for the period 1981–84 to study the World Bank. For this purpose she undertook field research in Washington, India, Algeria and Peru.

Publications: *Aid as Imperialism* (1981); *The Creation of World Poverty* (1981); *Aid: Rhetoric and Reality*, with Catherine Watson (1985).

He Liliang

Counsellor of the Department of International Organisations and Conferences, Ministry of Foreign Affairs, Beijing.

Born in 1926. A graduate of the Faculty of History, Moscow Institute of International Relations, 1958.

Madame He Liliang has served as Diplomatic Secretary and Counsellor in Ghana, Egypt and Canada as well as at the Chinese Permanent Mission to the United Nations in New York, 1960–76. She was Deputy Director of the Department of International Organisations of Conferences, Ministry of Foreign Affairs, Beijing, 1977–85.

Amir Jamal

Tanzanian politician, Minister in the President's Office.

Born in Dar es Salaam in 1922. Educated in Dar es Salaam and at the University of Calcutta.

Elected member of Tanganyika Legislative Council in 1958; Minister of Urban Local Government and Works 1959, of Communication, Power and Works 1960; Minister of State, President's Office, Directorate of Development, 1964; re-elected Member of Parliament 1965; Minister of Finance 1965–1972; Minister for Commerce and Industries 1972–75, of Finance and Economic Planning 1975–77, of Communications and Transport 1977–79, of Finance 1979–83.

He was appointed Minister without Portfolio in 1983.

Mr Jamal was a Member of the Brandt Commission 1977–80. He is on the

Governing Council of the Society for International Development and a Trustee of the Dag Hammeskjöld Foundation.

Peter Jankowitsch

Ambassador, Member of Parliament and International Secretary of the Socialist Party of Austria.

Born in Vienna 1933. Educated at University of Vienna. Entered the Austrian Foreign Service in 1957 and served in London and in Dakar, Senegal. Director of the office of Dr Kreisky, Chairman of the Socialist Party of Austria, 1967, and Director of the Cabinet of the Federal Chancellor, 1970–72. In 1972 Peter Jankowitsch was appointed Permanent Representative of Austria to the UN in New York and has led many Austrian delegations to international conferences. He was elected Chairman of the UN Committee for the Peaceful Uses of Outer Space 1972. He was Austrian Permanent Representative to the OECD from 1978–82.

Ambassador Jankowitsch was elected to Parliament in April 1983 and in December 1983 was appointed International Secretary of the Socialist Party of Austria.

Bruno Kreisky

Former Federal Chancellor of Austria (1970–83) and former Minister of Foreign Affairs (1959–66). Vice-President of the Socialist International.

Founder and President of the Vienna Institute for Development.

Born in Vienna 1911. Joined the Foreign Service in 1946 and served in the Federal President's Office 1951–53, becoming State Secretary for Foreign Affairs in the Federal Chancellery in 1953. He was elected to Parliament in 1956 and became Chairman of the Socialist Party of Austria in 1967, a post which he held until 1983.

His publications include: *The Challenge: Politics on the Threshold of the Atomic Age* (1963); *Aspects of Democratic Socialism* (1974); *Neutrality and Co-existence* (1975); *The Times We Live In: Reflections on International Politics* (1978).

Michael Manley

Leader of the Peoples' National Party. Former Prime Minister of Jamaica 1972–80. Vice-President of the Socialist International.

Born in Kingston 1923. Educated at Jamaica College and the London School of Economics.

Associate Editor, *Public Opinion* 1952–53; Sugar Supervisor, National Workers' Union, 1953–54; Island Supervisor and First Vice-President, 1955. Positions in numerous other unions and Labour Committees. Member of Senate 1962–67. Mr Manley was elected Leader of Peoples' National Party in February 1969. He was Prime Minister from March 1972–1980. Mr Manley also held the following portfolios: Minister of External Affairs 1972–75; Minister of Economic Affairs 1972–75; Minister of Defence 1972–80; Minister of Youth and Community Development 1974–75; Minister of National Mobilisation and Human Resources Development 1977–79; Minister of Information, Broadcasting and Culture 1978–80; Minister of Agriculture 1979–80.

Publications: *Politics of Change* (1974); *A Voice at the Workplace* (1975); *Search for Solutions* (1976); *Jamaica, Struggle in the Periphery* (1980).

Fred Sinowatz

Former Federal Chancellor (1983–86) and former Federal Vice-Chancellor of Austria (1981–83).

Born in Neufeld an der Leitha, Burgenland 1929. Educated at University of Vienna. Joined the Burgenland Provincial Government in 1953, proceeding to a ten year membership of the Burgenland Provincial Legis in 1961. He was President of the Legis from 1964 until 1971 when he was elected to Parliament, and became Minister of Education and Art (1971–83). Fred Sinowatz has also been Cultural Counsellor to the Burgenland Provincial Legis (1966–71); Party Secretary to the Burgenland Austrian Socialist Party (SPÖ) from 1961–78 and was appointed Deputy Chairman in 1978. He became a member of the SPÖ National Executive in 1981.

Dr Sinowatz is now the Chairman of the Austrian Socialist Party.

Thorvald Stoltenberg

Minister of Foreign Affairs to the Norwegian Labour government. Born in Oslo 1931. Studied International Law in United States, Austria, Finland and Switzerland, obtaining a degree in International Law from Oslo University.

Joined the Foreign Service in 1959 and served in San Francisco, Belgrade and Lagos.

His career with the Labour Party began as International Secretary of the Norwegian Federation of Trade Unions (1970–71, 1972–73 and 1981–83). Thorvald Stoltenberg has been State Secretary for the Foreign Ministry (1971–72), for the Ministry of Defence (1973–74), for the Ministry of Commerce and Shipping (1974–76) and for the Ministry of Foreign Affairs (1976–79). In 1968 he became Chairman of the Nordic Development Aid Group, and was Chairman of the Norwegian Consultative Council of the EEC, 1971–72 and 1976–79. He has twice been Vice-Chairman of the Norwegian Mission to the United Nations (1971–72 and 1976–79) and Defence Minister 1979–81.

Gabriel Valdes

A Chilean lawyer, President of the Christian Democrat Party of Chile, and board member of the Vienna Institute for Development.

PROGRAMME OF THE CONFERENCE

First Day: **Decolonisation and After**
Monday, 7 October 1985

Morning Session:
10.30–13.00

Welcoming Addresses:
  Bruno Kreisky
  President
  Vienna Institute for Development

  Humayun Gauhar
  Publisher and President
  South—The Third World Magazine

Introductory Statement by the Chairman:
  Peter Jankowitsch
  Ambassador, Member of Parliament (Austria)

Opening Address:
  Dr Fred Sinowatz
  Federal Chancellor of Austria

Independence and the Process of Decolonisation:
  Amir Jamal
  Minister in the President's Office (Tanzania)

The Caribbean Experience:*
  Michael Manley
  former Prime Minister (Jamaica)

Discussion

Afternoon Session:
15.00–18.00

Colonialism, Neo-Colonialism and Democratisation in Latin America:
  Gabriel Valdes
  Chairman, Christian-Democratic Party (Chile)

New China's Economic Development and the Current Structural Reforms:
  He Liliang
  Counsellor, Foreign Ministry (PR China)

The Asian Experience with particular reference to India, Pakistan and Bangladesh:
  Altaf Gauhar
  Editor-in-Chief, *South* (Pakistan)

Discussion

Evening:
19.00

Reception given by the Publisher and President of *South* magazine and Mrs Humayun Gauhar in honour of the participants.
The Federal Chancellor of Austria, Dr Fred Sinowatz, will be the guest of honour.
(Redoutensaal, Hofburg, Vienna)

Second Day: **Prospects for the Future**
Tuesday, October 8, 1985

Morning Session:
10.30–13.00

Introductory Statement by the Chairman:
    Thorvald Stoltenberg
    Leader, International Commission,
    Norwegian Labour Party

North–South Cooperation: Turning the Tide
    Bruno Kreisky
    former Federal Chancellor of Austria

Recovery and Development:*
    Professor Louis Emmerij
    Rector, Institute of Social Studies
    (The Netherlands)

Discussion

Afternoon Session:
15.00–18.00

Is Reform of the World Bank possible?
    Teresa Hayter
    Research Editor Greater London Council
    (United Kingdom)

Towards a New Internationalism:
    Professor Janez Stanovnik
    former Executive Secretary,
    UN Economic Commission for Europe
    (Yugoslavia)

Discussion

Summary and Conclusions
    The Chairman

*Indicates general subject, not the exact title.

The conference on 'Decolonisation and After—The Future of the Third World', was sponsored by the Vienna Institute for Development and *South* magazine. It was held in Vienna at the Redoutensaal, Hofburg, Josefsplatz 1, on 7–8 October 1986.

    An anticipated audience of 200 people turned out to be, in the end, 400 guests and participants. This was a gratifying development and rewarded the hard work put in by the organising team led by Dr Arne Haselbach, Director of the Vienna Institute for Development, and Clarence Da Gama Pinto, Chief of South's Conference and

Research Division. Also, actively involved from the VID were Dr Erich Andrlik and Ms Erika Elizabeth Grimm. We would also like to acknowledge the help of the two rapporteurs, Leslie Wolf-Phillips, Senior Lecturer in the Government Department at the London School of Economics and Alex Cockburn of *The Nation*, New York, in giving the proceedings of the seminar a final form.

LIST OF PARTICIPANTS

Michele Achilli	President, Istituto Cooperazione Economica Internazionale, Milano
Ahmed Maigida Adams	Permanent Mission of the Federal Republic of Nigeria, Vienna
Enrique Aguilar	Director, UN Information Service, Vienna
Aldo Ajello	Director, UNDP European Office, Geneva
Turan Akbas	Foreign student in Vienna (Turkey)
Michael Alexander	Ambassador, Embassy of the United Kingdom, Vienna
Mowaffak Allaf	Under-Secretary-General, Director-General of the United Nations Office, Vienna
Ali Abdul-Rahman Al-Muftah	Ambassador, Permanent Mission of the State of Qatar in the United Nations, Vienna
Sjaiful Amanullah	Counsellor, Permanent Mission of the Republic of Indonesia, Vienna
Erich Andrlik	Deputy Director, Vienna Institute for Development
Jacques Attali	Conseiller Spécial du Président de la République, Paris
Jean Pierre Ayrault	Secretary, IIASA, Laxenberg
Gerd Bacher	Generalintendant, O R F, Wien
Daoud Barakat	Permanent Observer of the Palestine Liberation Organisation to the United Nations, Vienna
Aroon Basak	Special Adviser to the Executive Director, UNIDO, Vienna
Hans Jörg Bauer	Head, UNIDO Investment Promotion Service—Vienna
Holger Bauer	Staatssekretär im Bundesministerium für Finanzen, Republik Österreich
Erich Becker-Boost	Director, Investment Cooperative Programme, UNIDO, Vienna
Bodo Beelitz	Ministerialrat, Bundesministerium für öffentliche Wirtschaft und Verkehr, Wien
Wolfgang Benedek	Vorsitzender, World University Service (Austria); Universitätsassistent, Institut für Völkerrecht und Internationale Beziehungen, Graz
Ahmed Ben Salah	Former Minister of Planning, National Economy and Education, Tunisia; Vice-President of the Board VID
Eugène Berg	Compagnie Française des Pétroles, Paris

Gabriele Berger-Boyer	Austrian Rail Engineering Ltd., Vienna
Herbert Berger	Sekretär, Arbeitsgemeinschaft 'Österreich—Dritte Welt' de SPÖ, Vienna
Burkhard Bischof	Journalist, *Die Presse*, Wien
Gerhard Bittner	Generalsekretär, Afro-Asiatisches Institut, Wien
Eli W. Bizic	Embassy of the United States of America, Vienna
Paul Blau	Professor, Publicist, Vienna
Karl Blecha	Bundesminister für Inneres, Republik Österreich
Patrick Blum	Correspondent, *Financial Times*, Vienna
Ernst Bobek	Sektionsleiter, Bundesministerium für Gesundheit und Umweltschutz, Vienna
Peter Bosshard	Nationalökonom, Zürich
Kemal Boztepe	Foreign student in Austria (Turkey)
Constance Bruckner	Entwicklungshilfe-Klub, Vienna
Hans Bürstmayr	Geschäftsführer, Österreichischer Entwicklungsdienst, Vienna
Cao Guisheng	Ambassador, Permanent Mission of the People's Republic of China, Vienna
Michael K. Carr	Embassy of Australia, Vienna
Giovanni Ceirano	Monsignor, Permanent Observer of the Holy See to the United Nations, Vienna
Chen Min	Shanghai Institute for International Studies, PR China
Chen Yuchu	Counsellor, Alternate Permanent Representative, Permanent Mission of China, Vienna
Trandafir Cocarla	Ambassador, Permanent Mission of the Socialist Republic of Romania to the UN, Vienna
Alexander Cockburn	Journalist, *The Nation*, New York
Markus Cornaro	Generalsekretariat, Bundesministerium für Auswärtige Angelegenheiten, Vienna
Barry Crowston	UNIDO, Vienna
Josef Czerny	Kammeramtsdirektor, Kammer für Arbeiter und Angestellte, Vienna
Adolf Czettel	Abgeordneter zum Nationalrat, Präsident, Österreichischer Arbeiterkammertag
Clarence Da Gama Pinto	Chief, Conference Division, *South* magazine
Margarida Da Gama Santos	CSDHA, United Nations, Vienna
Alexander De Faria	UNIDO, Vienna
Brigitte Dekrout	Oberrat, Bundesministerium für Auswärtige Angelegenheiten, Wien
Elfriede Dirnbacher	w. Hofrat, Bundespressedienst, Vienna
Johanna Dohnal	Staatssekretärin im Bundeskanzleramt, Republik Österreich
Margarete Dostal	Generalsekretär, Österreichische Orient-Gesselschaft—Hammer-Purgstall, Vienna
Gerhard Drekonja	Universitätsdozent, Klagenfurt
Jacques Du Guerny	CSDHA/AW, United Nations, Vienna

Fritz Edlinger	Generalsekretär, Gesselschaft für Österreichisch-Arabische Beziehungen, Wien
Kurt Eichinger	Generaldirektor, Plasser & Theurer, Wien
Issam El-Zaim	Regional and Country Studies Branch, UNIDO; Assistant Secretary-General, Association of Third World Economists
Louis Emmerij	Rector, Institute of Social Studies, The Hague; President-elect, OECD Development Centre, Paris
Hubert Feichtlbauer	Leiter der Presseabteilung, Bundeskammer der gewerblichen Wirtschaft, Vienna
Hans Fellinger	Pressereferent, Österreichischer Gewerkschaftsbund, Vienna
Heide-Marie Fenzl	Oberrat, Bundesministerium für Auswärtige Angelegenheiten, Vienna
Hertha Firnberg	Bundesminister a.D., Präsident, Ludwig-Boltzmann Gesselschaft, Vienna
Erich Fröschl	Direktor, Dr.-Karl-Renner-Institut, Vienna
Wolf Frühauf	Sektionsleiter, Bundesministerium für Wissenschaft und Forschung, Vienna
Brigitte Fuchs	Redakteurin, O R F—Hörfunk, Vienna
Harald Gardos	Generalsekretär, Österreichische UNESCO-Kommission,Vienna
Altaf Gauhar	Editor-in-Chief, *South*—The Third World Magazine
Humayun Gauhar	Publisher and President, *South*—The Third World Magazine
Bernhard Gebauer	Konrad-Adenauer-Stiftung, Vienna
Friedrich Gehart	Vorstandsdirektor, Österreichisches Credit-Institut, Vienna
Nellie Gehart	Intergovernmental Relations Section, UNIDO, Vienna
Dorata Gierytz	CSDHA/AW, United Nations, Vienna
Konrad Ginther	Universitätsprofessor, Institut für Völkerrecht und Internationale Beziehungen, Graz
Friedrich Gleissner	Leiter der Abteilung für Handelspolitik und Außenhandel, Bundeskammer der gewerblichen Wirtschaft, Vienna
Walter Göhring	Direktork, Institut für politische Bildung, Mattersburg
Gangadhar Gouri	Director, Division for Industrial Studies, UNIDO, Vienna
Jacqueline J. Granger	Society for International Development, Geneva
Erika Elisabeth Grimm	Head, Conference Department, Vienna Institute for Development
Horst Grunert	Ambassador, Embassy of the German Democratic Republic, Vienna
Karl Haas	Referat Wirtschaftshilfe, Bundeskammer der gewerblichen Wirtschaft, Vienna
Siegfried Haas	Researcher, Vienna Institute for Development

René Haguenauer	Chargé d'Affaires a.i., Embassy of Brazil, Vienna
Abbas Hamiye	Ambassador, Permanent Mission of Lebanon to UNIDO, Vienna
Elisabeth Hardegg	Österreichisches Komitee für UNICEF
Helmut Hartmeyer	Österreichischer Informationsdienst für Entwicklungspolitik, Vienna
Arne Haselbach	Director, Vienna Institute for Development
Ingomar Hauchler	Professor, Mitglied des Bundestages, Bundesrepublik Deutschland
Jürg Hauser	Professor, Stiftungsrat, SWISSAID, Schweiz
Hilde Hawlicek	Abgeordnete zum Nationalrat, Wien
Teresa Hayter	Research Editor, Greater London Council, United Kingdom
He Liliang	Counsellor, Foreign Ministry, People's Republic of China
Knut Hedemann	Ambassador, Permanent Mission of Norway to the United Nations, Vienna
Irene Heller	Auslandsbüro, Österreichische Nationalbank, Wien
John Hillberry	Bank of Credit and Commerce International (BCCI) London
Gerald Hinteregger	Generalsekretär, Bundesministerium für Auswärtige Angelegenheiten, Vienna
Jagdish R. Hiremath	Ambassador, Permanent Mission of India, Vienna
Georg Hoffmann-Ostenhof	Redakteur, *Arbeiter Zeitung*, Wien
William H. Holaday	Social scientist, Vienna
Otmar Höll	Österreichisches Institut für Internationale Politik, Laxenburg
Karin Höllriegl	'Save Africa's Future', Vienna
Milan Horacek	Mitglied des Bundestages, Bundesrepublik Deutschland
Manfred Horvat	Vorsitzender, Mattersburger Kreis für Entwicklungspolitik an den Österreichischen Universitäten Leiter, Außeninstitut, Technische Universität, Vienna
Othmar Huber	Generalsekretär, Österreichisches Lateinamerika Institut, Vienna
Hans Igler	Ehrenpräsident, Vereinigung Österreichischer Industrieller, Vienna
A. M. Im Hof	Stiftungsrätin, SWISSAID, Schweiz
M. Incisa Di Camerana	Chargé d'Affaires a.i., Permanent Mission of Italy, Vienna
Harald Irnberger	Chefredakteur, *Magazin*, Vienna
Waltraud Jakob	Redakteurin, *Wiener Zeitung*, Vienna
Amir Jamal	Minister in the President's Office, Tanzania; Member of the Board, VID
Odette Jankowitsch	Interagency Programme Coordination, UNIDO, Vienna

Peter Jankowitsch	Ambassador, Member of Parliament; Vice-President of the Board, VID
Manfred Kadits	Generaldirektor, Konsum Österreich, Vienna
Gerd Kaminski	Universitätsdozent, Ludwig-Boltzmann-Institut für China-und Südostasienforschung, Vienna
Jürg Känzig	Hilfswerk der Evangelischen Kirchen der Schweiz, Zürich
Bengt Karlsson	Head, Sectoral Studies Branch, UNIDO, Vienna
Christian Karsch	Verband der Versicherungsunternehmungen Österreichs, Vienna
Herta Kaschitz	CSDHA/AW, United Nations, Vienna
Mohammad Keiarishi	Ambassador of the Islamic Republic of Iran, Vienna
John Robert Kelso	Ambassador, Permanent Mission of Australia, Vienna
Mansour Khalid	Vice-President, Commission on 'Environmental Perspectives for the Year 2000'; Member of the Board VID, Sudan
Kushi M. Khan	Nationalökonom, Institut für Allgemeine Überseeforschung, Hamburg
Heinz Kienzl	Generaldirektor, Österreichische Nationalbank, Vienna
Ilan Knapp	Geschäftsführer, Österreichisches Institut für Berufsbildungsforschung, Vienna
Hanni Konitzer	Korrespondentin, *Frankfurter Allgemeine Zeitung*, Vienna
Ernesto Koref	Ambassador, Permanent Mission of Panama to the United Nations, Vienna
Valerie Koref	Permanent Mission of Panama to the United Nations, Vienna
Konrad Kovar	Bundesministerium für Auswärtige Angelegenheiten, Vienna
W. K. Kosek	Economic Advisor to the Counsellor, Embassy of the United States of America, Vienna
Helmut Kramer	Leiter, Österreichisches Institut für Wirtschaftsforschung, Vienna
Helmut Kramer	Universitätsprofessor, Institut für Politikwissenschaft, Universität Wien, Vienna
Bruno Kreisky	Former Federal Chancellor of Austria; President, Vienna Institute for Development
Christian Krepela	Legationsrat, Bundesministerium für Auswärtige Angelegenheiten, Vienna
Inga Krugmann-Randolf	Chefredakteurin, 'Entwicklung und Zusammenarbeit', Deutsche Stiftung für Internationale Entwicklung, Bonn
Adalbert Krims	Press officer, Vienna Institute for Development
Marian Krzak	Ambassador, Embassy of the Polish People's Republic, Vienna

Balakrishna Kulamarva	Journalist, Vienna
Abdulla Kusumaningbrang	Permanent Mission of the Republic of Indonesia, Vienna
Johannes P. Kyrle	Legationsrat, Kabinett des Bundesministers für Auswärtige Angelegenheiten, Wien
Martha Kyrle	Präsident, Österreichisches Komitee für UNICEF, Vienna
Erwin Lanc	Bundesminister a.D. Geschäftsführer, 'Z' Export- und Handelsbank, Vienna
Laszlo Lang	Institute for World Economics of the Hungarian Academy of Sciences, Budapest
Richard Langthaler	Österreichische Forschungsstiftung für Entwicklungshilfe, Vienna
Walter Larcher	Referat Internationale Rohstoffpolitik, Bundeskammer der gewerblichen Wirtschaft, Vienna
Gérard Latortue	Head, Negotiations Branch, UNIDO, Vienna
Albert Lauterbach	Professor, Author, Vienna
Paul Leifer	Gesandter, Bundesministerium für Auswärtige Angelegenheiten, Vienna
Li Mintao	Shanghai Institute for International Studies, PR China
Walter Lichem	Gesandter, Bundesministerium für Auswärtige Angelegenheiten, Vienna
Ulrich Loeser	Feasibility Studies Section, UNIDO, Vienna
Herbert Lust	Oberrat, Bundesministerium für Finanzen, Vienna
Dagmar Luuk	Mitglied des Bundestages, Bundesrepublik Deutschland
Joginder Malhotra	Professor, Universität Hamburg, Hamburg
Pierre-Emeric Mandl	Editor, *Carnets de l'Enfance*, UNICEF, Geneva
Michael Manley	Former Prime Minister of Jamaica; Leader of the Peoples' National Party
Otto Maschke	Gesandter, Bundesministerium für Auswärtige Angelegenheiten, Vienna
Kurt Mauler	Auslandsbüro, Österreichische Nationalbank, Vienna
Hans Mayr	Vizebürgermeister der Stadt Wien
Gottfried Mazal	Ministerialrat, Bundesministerium für Finanzen, Vienna
A. A. de Medeiros Patricio	Ambassador, Permanent Mission of Portugal, Vienna
Hayat Mehdi	Negotiations Branch, UNIDO, Vienna
Ivan Mejia-Solis	Ambassador, Permanent Mission of Nicaragua to the United Nations, Vienna
Ernst Michanek	Ambassador; Chairman, Dag Hammarkjöld Foundation, Uppsala; Member of the Board, VID, Sweden
Harald Miltner	Gesandter, Bundesministerium für Auswärtige Angelegenheiten, Vienna
Ralf-Matthias Mohs	Regional and Country Studies, UNIDO, Vienna

Edouard Molitor	Ambassador, Permanent Mission of Luxembourg, Vienna
Lothar Müller	Bundesrat, Landesparteisekretär der SPO, Innsbruck
Hermann Muegge	Acting Head, Regional and Country Studies, UNIDO, Vienna
Karl-Heinz Nachtnebel	Internationaler Sekretär, Österreichischer Gewerkschaftsbund, Vienna
Subrahmanjan Nanjundan	Former Deputy Director, Division of Industrial Operations, UNIDO
Carmen Nausner	'Save Africa's Future', Vienna
Elisabeth Nash	Journalist, Radio Austria International, Vienna
János Nagy	Ambassador of the Hungarian People's Republic, Vienna
Shadrack M. Ndam	Chief, Coordination Unit for the Industrial Development Decade for Africa, UNIDO, Vienna
Ernst Nedwed	Abgeordneter zum Nationalrat, Vienna
Ki Nemoto	Permanent Observer, Asian-African Legal Consultative Committee, Vienna
Marc Nerfin	President, International Foundation for Development Alternatives, Nyon, Switzerland
Moustapha Niasse	Former Minister of Foreign Affairs, Senegal; Member of the Board, VID
Stanko Nick	Counsellor, Alternate Permanent Representative, Permanent Mission of Yugoslavia to the United Nations, Vienna
Alain Nickels	Negotiations Branch, UNIDO, Vienna
Federico Nier-Fischer	Head, 'Inter-Press Service', Vienna Office
Eva Nowotny	Legationsrat, Kabinett des Bundeskanzlers, Bundeskanzleramt, Vienna
Ewald Nowotny	Abgeordneter zum Nationalrat, Universitätsprofessor, Wien
Thomas Nowotny	Gesandter, Bundesministerium für Auswärtige Angelegenheiten, Vienna
Ernst-Werner Nussbaum	Redakteur, ORF—Wirtschaftsredaktion, Wien
Jiri Obdrzalek	Permanent Mission of the CSSR to the United Nations, Vienna
Michael Obrowsky	Österreichische Forschungsstiftung für Entwicklungshilfe, Vienna
Esta Okoye	Foreign student in Austria (Kenya)
Kwame T. Opoku	UNIDO, Vienna
Helmut Ornauer	Geschäftsführer, Koordinierungsstelle der Österreichischen Bischofskonferenz für Internationale Entwicklung und Mission, Vienna
Enrique Oteiza	Director, United Nations Research Institute for Social Development, Geneva
Herwig Palme	Universitätsassistent, Interdisziplinäres Institut für Raumordnung, Wirtschaftsuniversität, Vienna

Julio Roberto Palomo Silva   Chargé d'Affaires a.i., Permanent Mission of Guatemala, Vienna

Mrs Sylvia Pauli   Chargé d'Affaires a.i., Embassy of Switzerland, Vienna

Gerhard Payr   Geschäftsführer, Österreichischer Informationsdienst für Entwicklungspolitik, Vienna

Ivo Pelicon   Editor-in-Chief, *Public Enterprise*, International Centre for Public Enterprises in Developing Countries, Ljubljana

Josef Pernerstorfer   Ministerialrat, Bundesministerium für Auswärtige Angelegenheiten, Vienna

H. Pfusterschmid-Hardtenstein   Botschafter, Direktor, Diplomatische Akademie, Wien

Michelangelo Pipan   Embassy of Italy, Vienna

Gonzalo Plaza   Director, OPEC News Agency, Vienna

Fritz Prechtl   Abgeordneter zum Nationalrat, Vorsitzender, Gewerkschaft der Eisenbahner, Vienna

Stanislaw Przygodzki   Ambassador, Permanent Mission of the Polish People's Republic to the International Organisations, Vienna

Hans Pusch   Leiter des Kabinetts des Bundeskanzlers, Vienna

Kunibert Raffer   Universitätsassistent, Institut für Wirtschaftswissenschaften, Universität Vienna

Alois Rastl   Austrian Rail Engineering Ltd., Vienna

Marielies Rehor   Oberrat, Bundesministerium für Auswärtige Angelegenheiten, Vienna

Alois Reitbauer   Botschafter, ehem. Generalsekretär des Bundesministeriums für Auswärtige Angelegenheiten, Vienna

Alfred Reiter   Direktor, Österreichische Investitionskredit AG, Vienna

Erich Reiter   Büro des Bundesministers für Landesverteidigung, Vienna

Victor A. Richardson   Negotiations Branch, UNIDO, Vienna

Phillipp Rieger   Nationalökonom, Vienna

Laura Q. del Rosario   Chargé d'Affaires a.i., Embassy of the Philippines, Vienna

Roberto De Rosenzweig-Diaz   Ambassador, Permanent Mission of Mexico, Vienna

Ramiro Ruggiero   Minister-Counsellor, Embassy of Italy, Vienna

Olof Rydbeck   Commissioner-General, UNRWA, Vienna

Tapio Saarela   Counsellor, Alternative Permanent Representative, Permanent Mission of Finland, Vienna

Erna Sailer   Botschafter, Vienna

Walter Sauer   Chefredakteur, *Entwicklungspolitische Nachrichten*, Vienna

Claudine Sauvain   Anthropologin, Stiftungsrat, SWISSAID, Schweiz

Karin Schicht	Vereinigung Österreichischer Industrieller, Vienna
Wolfgang Schindegger	Leiter, Institut für Internationale Zusammenarbeit, Vienna
Franz Schmid	Botschafter, Sektionsleiter, Bundesministerium für Auswärtige Angelegenheiten, Vienna
Renate Schneider	Österreichischer Informationsdienst für Entwicklungspolitik, Vienna
Peter Schnitt	Direktor, Exportakademie der Bundeskammer der gewerblichen Wirtschaft, Vienna
Otto Schönherr	Chefredakteur, Austria Presse Agentur, Vienna
Reinhard Schurawitzki	Rat, Bundesministerium für Wissenschaft und Forschung, Vienna
Gerhard Schuster	Bundesministerium für Familie, Jugend und Konsumentschutz, Vienna
Kurt-Peter Schütt	Forschungsinstitut der Friedrich-Ebert-Stifung, Bonn-Bad Godesberg
Hans Dietmar Schweisgut	Legationsrat, Büro des Bundesministers für öffentliche Wirtschaft und Verkehr, Vienna
Ingrid Seeman-Pelicon	Honorary Consulate of the Republic of Kenya, Vienna
Christa Seewann	Österreichischer Informationsdienst für Entwicklungspolitik, Vienna
Leticia Ramos Shahani	Assistant Secretary-General of the United Nations, DIESA/CSDHA, Vienna
Mohamed El-Taher Shash	Ambassador, Permanent Mission of the Arab Republic of Egypt to the UN, Vienna
Fred Sinowatz	Federal Chancellor of Austria
Stanislav Sokolenko	Division of Policy Coordination, UNIDO, Vienna
Song Zhensui	Chief, Section for Economic Cooperation Among Developing Countries, UNIDO, Vienna
Mr Gebran Soufran	Alternative Permanent Representative, Permanent Mission of Lebanon, Vienna
Marta Souza	Field Reports Monitoring Section, UNIDO, Vienna
Ulrich Stacher	Rat, Bundesministerium für Auswärtige Angelegenheiten, Vienna
Erhard Stackl	Redakteur, *Profil*, Vienna
Alcira Stania	Permanent Mission of Spain, Vienna
Janez Stanovnik	Member of the Collective Presidency of the Republic of Slovenia, Yugoslavia; former Executive Secretary, UN Economic Commission for Europe
Heribert Steinbauer	Abgeordneter zum Nationalrat, Vienna
Kurt Steyrer	Bundesminister für Gesundheit und Umweltschutz, Republik Österreich
Thorvald Stoltenberg	Leader, International Commission, Norwegian Labour Party; Member of the Board, VID
Michael Stricker	Redakteur, *Die Presse*, Vienna
Alfred Ströer	Leitender Sekretär des Österreichischen Gewerkschaftsbundes; Aufsichtsratsvorsitzender, Bank

	für Arbeit und Wirtschaft, Vienna
Enrique Suarez de Puga y Villegas	Ambassador, Permanent Mission of Spain, Vienna
Ernst Sucharipa	Gesandter, Leiter des Kabinetts des Bundesministers für Auswärtige Angelegenheiten, Vienna
Istvan Teszler	Embassy of the Hungarian People's Republic, Vienna
Albert Thabault	Ambassador, Permanent Mission of France to the United Nations, Vienna
Hans Thalberg	Botschafter; Direktor, Österreichisches Institut für internationale Politik, Laxenburg
Markus Timmler	Wirtschaftspublizist, Bonn–Bad Godesberg
Jonathan Kabo Umar	Ambassador, Permanent Mission of the Federal Republic of Nigeria, Vienna
Karl Vak	Generaldirektor, Zentralsparkasse und Kommerzialbank, Vienna
Gabriel Valdes	Chairman, Christian-Democratic Party, Chile; Member of the Board, VID
Ernst-Eugen Veselsky	Abgeordneter zum Nationalrat, Leitender Sekretär, Kammer für Arbeiter und Angestellte, Vienna
L. H. J. B. Van Gorkom	Ambassador, Permanent Mission of the Kingdom of the Netherlands, Vienna
Gerhard Wagner	Generaldirektor, Österreichische Länderbank, Wien
Elmar Walter	Sektionschef, Bundesministerium für Handel, Gewerbe und Industrie, Vienna
Peter Weinmar	Financial Manager, Vienna Institute for Development
Erich Weisbier	Direktor, Volkshilfe, Vienna
Thomas Wernley	Ambassador, Permanent Mission of Switzerland to the International Organisations, Vienna
Otto Winkler	Professor, Gründer und ehem. Leiter des Instituts für Internationale Zusammenarbeit, Vienna
Leslie Wolf-Phillips	Senior Lecturer in Political Science, London School of Economics, London
Ernst Woller	Wiener Bildungssekretär der SPÖ, Vienna
Axel Wüstenhagen	United Nations Information Service, Vienna
Yong Zheming	Shanghai Institute for International Studies, Peoples Republic of China
Kaarlo Juhana Yrjö-Koskinen	Ambassador, Permanent Mission of Finland, Vienna
Sergio Zampetti	Industrial Planning Section, UNIDO, Vienna
Otto Zellhofer	Ministerialrat, Bundesministerium für Wissenschaft und Forschung, Vienna
Karl Zemanek	Universitätsprofessor, Institut für Völkerrecht und Internationale Bezeihungen, Vienna

*Participants were invited in their personal capacities; institutional affiliations, functional titles, etc. are given for purposes of identification only.

THE VIENNA DECLARATION*
on
Cooperation for Development

Preamble

1. We, the citizens of many countries, rich and poor, have gathered together to consider what we regard, next to the maintenance of peace, and very much related to it, as the most urgent problem of our times. That problem is the one posed by the continuance in the second half of the twentieth century, of conditions of poverty, misery, disease and degradation for two-thirds of the human race. Not more than one third of the men and women of this world can be said to be adequately fed, clothed, housed and educated. And while the income of this fortunate third of humanity continues to increase, the underdeveloped world continues to stagnate, thus widening rapidly the already large gap that exists between the rich nations and the poor nations.

2. We regard the continuation of this state of affairs as immoral. The kind of inequality that exists between nations would never be permitted within the frontiers of a modern progressive nation-state; for the human conscience no longer tolerates the provision of luxuries for a few when the many are deprived of necessities. This inequality is avoided within the nation-state by continuous transfers of wealth from the rich to the poor individual and from the rich areas to the poorer ones. The world has become too small for fellow-feeling between man and man to stop at political frontiers.

3. The economic consequences of this international maldistribution of wealth are as harmful to the rich nations as to the poor. International trade is largely restricted to commerce between the developed nations; the underdeveloped nations have little part in it because they do not have the goods to sell in exchange for the commodities they so desperately need to buy. An increase in the production, and therefore in the purchasing power, of the two billion people in the underdeveloped countries would open up vast new horizons of international trade for the benefit no less of the rich nations than of the poor.

4. Politically, the increasing contrast between the rich and the poor is capable internationally of having the same disastrous consequences that inequality within nations has had among those who were not alert enough to check its growth in time. It is not the part of wisdom to allow conditions to continue, which, if not remedied, cannot but end in the destruction of the world order as we know it – in war, civil strife and chaos.

5. There are enough resources in the world today—and these resources are annually augmented—to wipe off poverty from the face of the earth. We believe that it is the inescapable obligation of the whole of humanity, whether rich or poor, to cooperate in this task. The primary responsibility for development must rest on the people of the underdeveloped countries themselves. It is their obligation to strain every nerve, to make every sacrifice, to draw out from their own meagre resources, human and

material, whatever may be required for the accomplishment of this task. Underdeveloped countries must plan and organise development; they must face the undoubtedly painful task of changing the structure of society wherever it stands in the way of progress; they must determinedly remove the vested interests which stand in the path of advancement; they must ensure that their scarce resources are not wasted in high consumption or unwise investment and they should pay adequate attention to the consequences of a rapid rise in population.

6. It is however beyond doubt that the resources of the underdeveloped countries, whether in men or money, are insufficient to produce an effective rate of growth. We consider it the obligation of the developed countries to aid this task of development by providing to their less fortunate brothers the resources they lack.

7. The resources required for the creation of wealth are the tools of production and the knowledge to put them to use. The tools can be provided, firstly by enabling the underdeveloped countries freely to sell their goods, by removing the barriers that are now placed in their way in the markets of the developed countries. They have, secondly, to be provided by rapidly increasing programmes of capital assistance so that non-commercial capital transfers reach the minimum level of one per cent of the total combined national incomes of the developed countries. The knowledge can be provided by increasing substantially the programmes of technical assistance.

8. We recommend that the governments of all nations pledge to each other that they will, during the United Nations Development Decade, do whatever they can, to develop the underdeveloped parts of the world so that humanity may be rid of the age-old but now totally unnecessary curse of poverty.

I. Problems of Development

The poverty of the peoples of Asia, Africa, and Latin America is the central problem of our times. Partly as the heritage of colonial exploitation, partly as the by-product of increased population, partly because of the poverty of capital and education, the standard of living of families in developing countries is tragically low—only a tiny fraction of that of families in the rich countries.

What is worse, the gap has been progressively widening.

For every reason—political, economic, and moral—the challenge presented by this gap should be met by a partnership to extend prosperity to all peoples. But as yet the world—particularly the more fortunate peoples—is only dimly aware of what is needed to meet this challenge.

The partnership between the haves and the have-nots must be sought in expanding trade in order to enable the developing countries to earn their own way as far and as soon as possible; in increased aid by the advanced nations— in goods, in capital, and in shared skills and in the determination by the developing countries to create modern societies characterised by vastly expanded agricultural and industrial production, and above all by social justice.

II. Trade

To enable the developing countries to acquire the capital for their development, they must be allowed

(1) to export the largest possible volume of goods,

(2) under terms which yield them the largest possible income.

Barriers to trade on the part of the advanced nations now prevent realising this first objective. Indeed, economic alliances, customs unions, common markets, and similar regional organisations, though desirable in their essential concept, could impair unity if they raised walls against products of the developing countries or discriminate in favour of the products of one developing country at the expense of another.

Moreover, the instability of prices of many raw materials and agricultural products of underdeveloped countries has created a steady deterioration in the terms of trade. The poor countries are hurt, and the rich countries get richer.

Accordingly, we call for the adoption of the following principles:

1. The developed countries must progressively lower their tariffs—tariffs, quotas, taxes—against the products of developing countries. This liberalisation should include not only traditional agricultural and raw materials but, increasingly, manufactured goods. The liberalisation must be brought about by individual developed nations, by customs unions, and by the industrialised nations as a whole.

2. The developed countries must assume responsibility for protecting the traditional exports of underdeveloped countries from the consequences of violent price fluctuations. Commodity agreements aimed at stabilising income or prices need to be expanded. An international insurance fund, which would adequately compensate against harmful price fluctuations and permit the planning of production for full consumption, should be established.

3. The developing countries must be allowed to depart from the principles of free trade for a time sufficient for them to develop needed industries including those in aid of agriculture. Regional organisations can serve a useful purpose by recommending plans for locating new industries where they will permit the most effective use of labour and materials.

4. The advanced countries must pursue vigorous policies of full employment, maximum growth, and stable currencies, not only for their own benefit but in order to provide the widest possible market for the goods of developing countries.

III. Aid

The needs of the developing countries for foreign capital over and above export earnings are enormous for the period until they can grow by themselves. Our goal is the fastest possible self-sustaining growth.

The developed nations should jointly agree to the goal of providing to the underdeveloped world a minimum of one per cent of their gross national product in public loans, grants, and technical assistance (as distinct from public or private capital investments or credits on commercial terms). Because this will still do little to close the gap between the rich and the poor, we hope that it may be supplemented by resources released by progressive disarmament.

The aid programmes of the developed nations are complicated by the balance of payments difficulties confronting some of them. Those of the developed countries which have accumulated large monetary reserves must provide substantial credits. Furthermore, these must be on terms which permit them to be spent in countries whose balance of payments difficulties make it easier to supply goods than credits.

To encourage private investment in underdeveloped countries on terms that are fair, we recommend new arrangements whereby the receiving country guarantees against political risks, in return for the gradual transfer of the investment from the investing countries within a specified time limit.

Economic assistance from the developed countries should include grants, particularly for technical assistance, surveys, and education; long-term low-interest loans, repayable in local currency, for the economic infrastructure, such as ports; and 'harder' loans, as from the World Bank. To the greatest extent aid should be channelled through the United Nations.

More imaginative arrangements for channelling surplus foods through to hungry people, such as school lunch programmes or work-projects, should be expanded.

Technical assistance missions give a constructive opportunity for one less developed country to help another.

No political condition should be attached to aid. But the developing country must frame a coherent plan, drawing on the cooperative effort of all social groups, to raise incomes and make them more equal, to increase the literacy rate, and to improve its system of taxation and land tenure.

IV. *Armament Costs as an Obstacle to Development Assistance*

Even partial disarmament could bring a tremendous lift to worldwide standards of living by releasing material resources.

Plans for a wise and equitable utilisation of possible savings from disarmament should be made immediately.

Additional gains from disarmament are:

(1) A political climate conducive to international cooperation;
(2) The release of high-quality human resources—scientists, administrators and gifted young people.

V. *Structural Reforms in Developing Countries*

1. For rapid economic, social and cultural development it is essential to utilise for productive purposes in the most effective way the available human and natural resources for the benefit of all the people of the country.
2. It is necessary to create favourable conditions by continually improving opportunities and by promoting equality of opportunities for education and productive work and removing all obstacles based on caste, custom, colour, creed, language, or regional, economic or legal restrictions which may hamper the fullest productive utilisation of all resources, by the people, for all the people.
3. It is also necessary to promote the growth of the scientific outlook and of scientific

research in its widest sense to supply the concept of objective validity based on relevant data and correct reasoning as the guiding principle in making decisions. This is the heart of the problem of modernisation.

4. We therefore recommend the adoption and speedy implementation of a long-range comprehensive policy of planning for national development based on essential reforms in agriculture, education, fiscal policy and social-economic and political institutions in accordance with the principles enunciated above.

5. Information, ideas, advice, economic aid and technical and scientific assistance from outside are essential and are urgently needed, but the principal effort for development must come from the people themselves. The encouragement and the promotion of voluntary, democratic, non-governmental agencies for social, economic and cultural development should be an integral part of national planning in addition to direct governmental efforts. Foreign aid should be purposeful and efficiently directed to promote modernisation and the growth of democratic institutions.

6. Land reform is needed in many regions in order to avoid the inability of the farmer to invest in their work for lack of land, while other land remains totally or partially unused because of absentee ownership. In any case, land reforms should be implemented on the double basis of social justice and economic efficiency and usury and share cropping should be regarded as obstacles to progress in agriculture.

7. The cooperative movement is of vital importance in the transformation of the economic, educational, and social structure of developing countries, particularly countries moving from subsistence to market economies and as a unique, practical and indispensable channel through which the people can help themselves. In a mixed economy private enterprise would play a useful part and adequate credit should be made available to independent businessmen to enable them to compete with larger establishments.

It is recommended that legally and eventually constitutional measures should be taken in order to encourage and develop the cooperative movement. It is also recommended that part of the foreign aid programme be channelled through cooperative institutions directly to the people through their free genuine credit unions and other cooperative associations which are controlled and administered by their members. Where these cooperative associations do not exist or are in need of further development, it is recommended that some foreign aid funds be used to encourage their creation and development.

8. It is necessary to ensure that workers can secure an adequate share of the fruits of their labour in accordance with the principles of equity and social justice. Every effort should be made to ensure freedom of association and to encourage trade union movements directed to increasing production, technical training and improvements, social advance and rapid national development.

9. It is necessary to direct attention to the importance of demographic problems in relation to economic development and national planning.

VI. *Educational and Cultural Relations*

1. There is urgent need to establish a nation-wide system of education with the widest possible base at the primary stage suited to the needs of the country and within its

financial resources. While we believe that the standards of university education in the developing countries should be maintained and improved, we urge that immediate and greater emphasis should be placed on training in public administration, technical education, and on the teaching of skilled trades with a view to the successful implementation of development plans. In order to facilitate this task, we recommend that more support should be given to technical colleges and commercial schools, and for the provision of scholarships for technical training overseas.

2. There is also urgent need of establishing and supporting national and regional scientific and technological institutions to promote facilities for advanced studies and research for the people of the developing countries, with the active collaboration of scientists and technologists from advanced countries who would come to work in such institutions for suitable periods. The aim must be to create a sufficiently large community of professional scientists to facilitate free interchange of ideas and experience, to provide the stimulus of objective scientific criticism, and to promote the growth of the spirit of science and the modernisation of society.

3. We recommend that all national development plans should include an account of social and cultural conditions in the developing country preparing the programme, as well as indicating its economic requirements and proposals for meeting them.

4. We recommend that the public in the developed countries should be made aware of the character, the needs and the cultural heritage of the developing countries by the widest possible use of educational and cultural agencies, that is exchange of teachers and lecturers, translations of classical and modern publications by African, Asian and Latin American authors, by founding of institutes for African, Asian, and Latin American studies, exhibitions of art and other local products and by means of all the channels of publicity. At the same time educational efforts should be undertaken in the developing countries to create a climate of cooperation. In particular, efforts should be made to strengthen international understanding and peaceful cooperation, based on objective and truthful information about peoples of different regions of the world.

5. In order to promote partnership in cultural cooperation between developed and developing countries, we recommend the mutual adoption of towns, schools, youth organisations, cooperatives and other non-governmental organisations by corresponding institutions.

6. We recommend that all technicians, voluntary workers and other persons from developed countries proceeding to work in developing countries should undergo a course of study about the social conditions, cultural backgrounds and history of the country to which they are sent. And care should be taken to select personnel capable of quick adaptation to local conditions.

7. We are fully aware of the role of education in bringing about economic and social development. In particular, programmes in the field of adult education for the promotion of literacy, vocational training and health instruction should be extended. We recommend organisations and governments to support to their utmost the work of UNESCO in the sphere of planning and improving education at all levels.

8. We recommend that the developed countries utilise the idealism of their youth in their assistance programmes to the developing countries both through governmental and privately sponsored programmes. The eventual possibility of multilateral enterprises of this type, perhaps under the auspices of the United Nations, should be ascertained, because of the greater impact of multilateral undertakings.

*In 1961, Bruno Kreisky, then Austrian Minister of Foreign Affairs, convened a conference of eminent personalities from industrialized and developing countries with a view to finding new forms and invigorating cooperation to develop the underdeveloped parts of the world and to rid humanity of the age-old curse of poverty.

The 'Conference for Economic Cooperation and Partnership', which met in July 1962, and the historic document adopted on this occasion, led to the creation of the Vienna Institute for Development and to almost twenty-five years of intensive efforts under his leadership to pursue these goals.

INDEPENDENT STATES: FORMER TRUST AND NON-SELF-GOVERNING TERRITORIES* THAT HAVE ATTAINED INDEPENDENCE

Independent State	Year of Independence	Former Administering Authority (and former name)
Algeria	1962	France
Angola	1975	Portugal
Antigua	1981	United Kingdom
Bahamas	1973	United Kingdom
Barbados	1966	United Kingdom
Belize	1981	United Kingdom
Benin	1960	France (Dahomey)
Botswana	1966	United Kingdom (Bechuanaland)
Brunei	1983	United Kingdom
Burundi	1962	Belgium[1]
Cameroon, United Republic of	1960	France and United Kingdom[2]
Cape Verde	1975	Portugal
Central African Republic	1960	France (Ubangi-Shari)
Chad	1960	France
Comoros	1975	France
Congo	1960	France (Middle Congo)
Cyprus	1960	United Kingdom
Democratic Kampuchea	1953	France (Cambodia)
Democratic Yemen	1967	United Kingdom (Aden)
Djibouti	1977	France (Territory of the Afars and the Issas)
Dominica	1978	United Kingdom
Equatorial Guinea	1968	Spain (Fernando Poo and Rio Muni)
Fiji	1970	United Kingdom
Gabon	1960	France
Gambia	1965	United Kingdom
Ghana	1957	United Kingdom[3]
Grenada	1974	United Kingdom
Guinea	1958	France
Guinea-Bissau	1974	Portugal
Guyana	1966	United Kingdom
Indonesia	1949	Netherlands (Dutch Indies)

Independent State	Year of Independence	Former Administering Authority (and former name)
Ivory Coast	1960	France
Jamaica	1962	United Kingdom
Kenya	1963	United Kingdom
Kiribati	1979	United Kingdom (Gilbert Islands)
Lao People's Democratic Republic	1953	France (Laos)
Lesotho	1966	United Kingdom (Basutoland)
Madagascar	1960	France
Malawi	1964	United Kingdom (Nyasaland)
Malaysia	1957	United Kingdom (Malaya)[4]
Mali	1960	France (French Sudan)
Malta	1964	United Kingdom
Mauritania	1960	France
Mauritius	1968	United Kingdom
Morocco	1956	France
Mozambique	1975	Portugal
Nauru	1968	Australia[5]
Niger	1960	France
Nigeria	1960	United Kingdom[2]
Papua New Guinea	1975	Australia (Papua and the Trust Territory of New Guinea)
Rwanda	1962	Belgium[1]
Saint Christopher and Nevis	1983	United Kingdom
Saint Lucia	1979	United Kingdom
Saint Vincent and the Grenadines	1979	United Kingdom
Samoa	1962	New Zealand (Trust Territory of Western Samoa)
São Tomé and Príncipe	1975	Portugal
Senegal	1960	France
Seychelles	1976	United Kingdom
Sierra Leone	1961	United Kingdom
Singapore	1965	United Kingdom[4]
Solomon Islands	1978	United Kingdom
Somalia	1960	Italy and United Kingdom[6]
Suriname	1975	Netherlands (Dutch Guiana)
Swaziland	1968	United Kingdom
Tanzania, United Republic of	1961	United Kingdom[7]

Independent State	Year of Independence	Former Administering Authority (and former name)
Togo	1960	France (Trust Territory of Togoland)
Trinidad and Tobago	1962	United Kingdom
Tunisia	1956	France
Tuvalu	1978	United Kingdom (Ellice Islands)
Uganda	1962	United Kingdom
Upper Volta (Burkina Faso)	1960	France
Vanuatu	1980	France and United Kingdom (New Hebrides)
Viet Nam	1945	France
Zaire	1960	Belgium (Congo)
Zambia	1964	United Kingdom (Northern Rhodesia)
Zimbabwe	1980	United Kingdom (Southern Rhodesia)

*Territories for which trusteeship agreements were entered into by the United Nations and those which were listed by the General Assembly as non-self-governing.

[1] The Trust Territory of Ruanda-Urundi under Belgian administration became the independent States of Rwanda and Burundi in 1962.

[2] The Trust Territory of the Cameroons under French administration became independent as Cameroon in 1960. In 1961, in the Trust Territory of the Cameroons under British administration. Southern Cameroons voted to join Cameroon and Northern Cameroons voted to join Nigeria.

[3] The British Gold Coast Colony and Protectorate united with the Trust Territory of Togoland under British administration in 1957 to form Ghana.

[4] In 1963 the Federation of Malaya became Malaysia following the admission to the new federation of Singapore, Sabah (North Borneo) and Sarawak. Singapore became independent in 1965.

[5] The Trust Territory of Nauru was administered by Australia on behalf of the joint administering authority of Australia, New Zealand and the United Kingdom.

[6] The Trust Territory of Somaliland under Italian administration united with British Somaliland in 1960 to form Somalia.

[7] The Trust Territory of Tanganyika became independent in 1961, and Zanzibar became independent in 1963. Following the ratification in 1964 of Articles of Union between Tanganyika and Zanzibar, the United Republic of Tanganyika and Zanzibar changed its name to the United Republic of Tanzania.

UN DECLARATION ON THE GRANTING OF INDEPENDENCE TO COLONIAL COUNTRIES AND PEOPLES

Adopted by United Nations General Assembly

On 14 December 1960 the General Assembly of the United Nations adopted by an overwhelming majority a 'Declaration on the Granting of Independence to Colonial Countries and Peoples' in which it solemnly proclaimed 'the necessity of bringing to a speedy and unconditional end colonialism in all its forms and manifestations.'

By this decision the United Nations gave fresh impetus to the historic development which, during the life of the Organisation, has seen nearly 50 dependent territories, including United Nations trust territories, gain sovereign independence and many others advance to the threshold of statehood.

In his opening statement at the 1976 session of the Special Committee of 24 on Decolonisation, Secretary-General Kurt Waldheim said that, while the United Nations rejoiced at the progress achieved, it must be mindful of the fact that some 17 million people in various parts of the world remained under alien rule. Intensified effort must be made to meet the challenge of the changing dimensions of some of the colonial problems. For the millions of people still remaining under colonial rule, the Declaration remained an unfulfilled promise which was the duty of the United Nations to realise, the Secretary-General declared.

The full text of the Declaration is given below.

The General Assembly,

Mindful of the determination proclaimed by the peoples of the world in the Charter of the United Nations to reaffirm faith in fundamental human rights, in the dignity and worth of the human person, in the equal rights of men and women and of nations large and small and to promote social progress and better standards of life in larger freedom,

Conscious of the need for the creation of conditions of stability and well-being and peaceful and friendly relations based on respect for the principles of equal rights and self-determination of all peoples, and of universal respect for, and observance of, human rights and fundamental freedoms for all without distinction as to race, sex, language or religion.

Recognizing the passionate yearning for freedom in all dependent peoples and the decisive role of such peoples in the attainment of their independence,

Aware of the increasing conflicts resulting from the denial of or impediments in the way of the freedom of such peoples, which constitute a serious threat to world peace.

Considering the important role of the United Nations in assisting the movement for independence in trust and non-self-governing territories,

Recognizing that the peoples of the world ardently desire the end of colonialism in all its manifestations,

Convinced that the continued existence of colonialism prevents the development of international economic cooperation, impedes the social, cultural and economic development of dependent peoples and militates against the United Nations ideal of universal peace,

Affirming that peoples may, for their own ends, freely dispose of their natural wealth and resources without prejudice to any obligations arising out of international economic cooperation, based upon the principle of mutual benefit, and international law,

Believing that the process of liberation is irresistible and irreversible and that, in order to avoid serious crises, an end must be put to colonialism and all practices of segregation and discrimination associated therewith,

Welcoming the emergence in recent years of a large number of dependent territories into freedom and independence, and recognizing the increasingly powerful trends towards freedom in such territories which have not yet attained independence.

Convinced that all peoples have an inalienable right to complete freedom, the exercise of their sovereignty and the integrity of their national territory,

Solemnly proclaims the necessity of bringing to a speedy and unconditional end colonialism in all its forms and manifestations;

And to this end

Declares that:

1. The subjection of peoples to alien subjugation, domination and exploitation constitutes a denial of fundamental human rights, is contrary to the Charter of the United Nations and is an impediment to the promotion of world peace and cooperation.
2. All peoples have the right to self-determination; by virtue of that right they freely determine their political status and freely pursue their economic, social and cultural development.
3. Inadequacy of political, economic, social or educational preparedness should never serve as a pretext for delaying independence.
4. All armed action or repressive measures of all kinds directed against dependent peoples shall cease in order to enable them to exercise peacefully and freely their right to complete indepedence, and the integrity of their national territory shall be respected.
5. Immediate steps shall be taken, in trust and non-self-governing territories or all other territories which have not yet attained independence, to transfer all powers to the peoples of those territories, without any conditions or reservations, in accordance with their freely expressed will and desire, without any distinction as to race, creed or colour, in order to enable them to enjoy complete independence and freedom.
6. Any attempt aimed at the partial or total disruption of the national unity and the territorial integrity of a country is incompatible with the purposes and principles of the Charter of the United Nations.
7. All states shall observe faithfully and strictly the provisions of the Charter of the United Nations, the Universal Declaration of Human Rights and the present Declaration on the basis of equality, non-interference in the internal affairs of all states and respect for the sovereign rights of all peoples and their territorial integrity.

INDEX